meQuilibrium

meQuilibrium

14 Days to Cooler, Calmer, and Happier

**Jan Bruce, Andrew Shatté, Ph.D.,
and Adam Perlman, M.D., M.P.H.**

HARMONY
BOOKS · NEW YORK

Published in the United States by Harmony Books, an imprint of
the Crown Publishing Group, a division of Random House LLC,
a Penguin Random House Company, New York.
www.crownpublishing.com

Harmony Books is a registered trademark, and the Circle colophon
is a trademark of Random House LLC.

Library of Congress Cataloging-in-Publication Data
Bruce, Jan.
   Mequilibrium : 14 days to cooler, calmer, and happier / Jan
Bruce, Andrew Shatté, Ph.D., and Adam Perlman, M.D.
       pages cm
1. Resilience (Personality trait) 2. Adjustment (Psychology)
I. Shatté, Andrew. II. Perlman, Adam. III. Title.
BF698.35.R47B78 2014
158.1—dc23

5658 5242   04/15   2014023052

ISBN 978-0-8041-3849-9
eBook ISBN 978-0-8041-3850-5

Printed in the United States of America

Book design: Nicola Ferguson
Jacket design: Jess Morphew
Jacket art: Shutterstock

10 9 8 7 6 5 4 3 2 1

First Edition

I'd like to dedicate our book to my children, Jessica and Oliver, who first started me on my journey of balancing and made it so joyful and rewarding. And first and foremost to my husband, Richard, who showed me the meaning of having it all and made it a reality.

—*Jan Bruce*

To my parents, Betty and Lloyd, who taught me the importance of meaning and purpose. And to my wife, Veronica, and my children, Vivien and Julian, who gave it expression.

—*Andrew Shatté*

I'd like to dedicate this book to my wife, Laurice, and children, Sarah, Ben, Matt, Rebecca, and Charlie; they keep me balanced and remind me of what is really important in life.

—*Adam Perlman*

Contents

PART THREE. **Keep It Going**

Acknowledgments

To those who saw the wisdom in what we were building and gave us the backbone to stay with it: Laurie Coots, who has helped us see the disruptiveness in our brand; Richard Pine, who saw it, shaped it, stayed with us; Wright Steenrod and David Jones, who shared our belief in the power of consumers to change the course of health care and in our ability to help get consumers into the driver's seat of their personal well-being; Terri Trespicio, who shaped so many of our words and made our lessons practical not preachy; Robin Streit and Elisa Corra, who steadfastly enabled our development; and Teresa Keever for her research assistance.

Heartfelt thanks and appreciation to Debra Goldstein, our unflappable writer, whose talent and tenacity brought our book to life; to Heather Jackson, our editor, for her enthusiasm for our project and constant attention to its progress; and to our editorial director, Diana Baroni, for her support and smarts.

Foreword

Welcome to the wellness revolution! Just by picking up this book, you're officially part of it.

By "revolution," I mean that our culture is finally waking up to the fact that if we want to be happy and healthy, we need to think bigger. For far too long, too many people turned to quick-fix answers in their health and weight struggles. It was practically the American way: We tried fad diets to lose weight, swallowed pills to lift our mood, or self-medicated with food or alcohol to calm our worried minds. None of it worked. As a society, we just got fatter, sicker, unhappier, and more stressed.

Why? Because, as Jan Bruce, Dr. Andrew Shatté, and Dr. Adam Perlman reveal in this groundbreaking book, we were focusing on the fleeting solutions rather than the underlying problem. We didn't need to change what was going on in our lives and surroundings so much as we needed to dig deeper and change what was going on within *ourselves*.

For the past two decades, I have practiced Functional Medicine and written books based on its principles, which focus on the pursuit of health rather than the treatment of disease. Every ailment has a deeper cause, and I treat patients based on the whole person, to root out that cause. We look at everything; not just what their blood work says, but how they eat and, most pointedly, how they deal with stress. If I were to continue to treat just their symptoms and overlook this complex web underneath, my patients would be back in my office in less than a year. This whole-person approach challenges the core beliefs of those who still buy into the "take a pill" (aka quick-fix) approach. Ironically, as millions of patients and readers can attest, when you focus on building health, you automatically eradicate disease and shed excess weight. It really is that simple.

Stress is the ultimate health robber, causing or worsening 95 percent of all illness. Having a calm mind is so integral to health that it is actually one of my seven Keys to UltraWellness. Not only does stress make us sick, but it prevents us from healing. It floods our body with hormones that cause us to pack on deadly belly fat and sabotages our weight-loss efforts. We are seeing an epidemic of stress-related disorders in our society, ranging from depression to dementia, anxiety to obesity. Big Pharma and Big Food love the stress epidemic, as millions of Americans rely on pills, sugar, and caffeine to "feel better." But as I've written about extensively in my books, the answer doesn't sit on drugstore shelves—it's within our minds!

That's where this life-changing book comes in; meQuilibrium is the first program of its kind that goes way beyond the "take a pill" approach to stress management. No more trying to eradicate stress with fruitless and fleeting measures. I'm betting you've tried that already! Just as successful weight loss and vibrant health can be yours by changing your lifestyle, successful stress management can be yours if you learn how to change your thought style. And that is precisely what this book will teach you to do. This powerful program is a radical new way of approaching how you think and react to stress. The authors—three warriors of wellness in their respective industries—have brought together the principles of Functional Medicine, positive psychology, and proven real-world strategies to create a systemic approach for achieving the peace of mind and health you're seeking.

You don't have to suffer needlessly from the perils of stress for one more day. You don't have to feel tired, drained, or depressed, or struggle with weight or health issues. There is a better, healthier, happier life waiting for you. Take the leap for 14 days, and it's yours!

Mark Hyman, M.D.

Introduction

Life can be stressful.

You don't need us to tell you that. And you probably don't need us to tell you the reasons why. Mile-long to-do lists, demanding workloads and pressing deadlines, having to do more with less, juggling our kids' complex schedules, caring for aging parents, relationship conflicts . . . even reading this list can cause stress!

It's not news that chronic stress takes a toll on the quality of our lives. It muddies our thinking, impairs our judgment, damages our health and our relationships, and, perhaps most pointedly, makes us miserable.

Up until now, the prevailing wisdom has been to allay stress with a pill, a massage, a vacation. But we're not here to teach you how to relax. We won't promise you that the answer is a new breathing technique or suggest you just power off your devices for an afternoon. Certainly, these quick fixes offer a welcome respite in the moment, but the results are fleeting and leave you right back where you started. "Stress relief" isn't our goal. We're looking to create long-term, deep-rooted, sustainable calm, no matter what life throws at you.

Here's the short list of what else we're not going to suggest you do to get rid of stress:

Find a new job
Work less
Move to a more peaceful environment
Leave your relationship
Slash your to-do list
Invest in a complicated time-organization system
Give up anything you love to do

Why? Because you actually *can't* annihilate stress. It's not possible; stress is an undeniable factor generated by busy, modern lives. But you *can* learn to manage it peacefully—and you don't need to radically change your life to do so. If you think about it, stress often stems from trying to balance the things we value most: our family involvement, work, friends, caring for our health, the activities that bring us joy. So you see, this isn't about getting rid of stress but rather shifting your *response* to stress. And that changes everything. In just 14 days, we'll teach you a new way to respond and, in turn, a new way to live.

It's nearly impossible to avoid traffic jams, demanding bosses, willful teenagers, financial pressures, health glitches, and other challenges that make up the multistranded stress web of a modern life. But you can control the thinking that you're bringing to these encounters, which dictates your stress response. That's the key, because that's where you'll get your leverage. When you start to reframe your reactions to these encounters, you build up the most critical antidote to stress: resilience.

Create a new internal operating system for yourself and suddenly it won't matter that the stressors haven't changed, because *you* will have changed. You will find that you can do a lot of things you never thought you could, such as focus better at work, problem-solve more efficiently and effectively, and communicate more clearly. Your fatigue and malaise will begin to dissipate, and you'll feel able and inspired to make the healthy lifestyle changes that will further reduce your stress levels. Best of all, you'll be able to direct the energy you've been spending on worry, anxiety, guilt, sadness, and frustration into activities that are truly rewarding: deepening relationships, engaging in fulfilling work, or even just enjoying your busy life instead of watching it whiz by.

In 2010, we founded meQuilibrium, a personalized, interactive coaching system designed to provide people with proven, measurable methods to increase their stress resilience. Drawing on our individual areas of expertise, we married the systemic, whole-person approach of integrative medicine with the science of resilience and the tenets of positive psychology to create a methodology that attacks stress on every level. The program provided a revolutionary approach to stress, shifting the conversation from how people can eradicate it to how they can markedly improve their ability to handle it. It delivered cutting-edge skills to help them regain—and keep—control over their busy lives.

The efficacy of this unique program has been demonstrated in nine research trials. In just 60 days, meQuilibrium users reported significant improvements in how they felt physically and emotionally, their ability to focus and manage anxiety, and their sense of satisfaction with their lives. Since that time, many leading corporations and institutions have signed on, offering the program to their employees, and the number of users continues to grow daily.

But we're on a mission, and we're not stopping there. While the program is available to anyone, and we encourage you to visit www.mequilibrium.com to learn more, we wanted to offer a way for even more people to take back control of their lives. And, we wanted to get you there faster than 60 days.

We wrote this book as a way to deliver the key skills you'll need in a supercharged 14-day program. Think of this as a whole-life reboot—a complete upgrade of your internal operating system that improves how you think, feel, and live. This book's plan was scientifically designed to tackle the core components of stress management that are proven to give you the most bang for your buck. In other words, hit these 14 skills, and you'll quickly create a network of positive changes in every area of your life. We spent years designing our methodology, testing it repeatedly to ensure its efficacy, so that all you have to do is dedicate a few minutes each day to resetting your stress response—the rest happens automatically.

You'll learn to peacefully coexist with your stress and become happier, calmer, healthier, more productive, and in control of your life—and you'll do it *fast*. The last thing anyone who is stressed wants is a complicated, time-consuming program that causes more stress! The skills are quick and easy to adopt, so you'll begin to feel relief almost immediately. At the same time, they target the thinking and other underlying factors that generate stress in the first place, so the results are long-term.

Part 1 of the book will give you an overview of the program: what it is, how it was created, and, most important, why it works. While we know you're eager to get started on the change-your-life fast track right away, we strongly encourage you to not skip reading part 1, as it lays important groundwork for the program that follows.

Part 2 is a day-by-day breakdown of the program. Each day's material should take you about 15 minutes to read and put into practice. You don't need to follow the plan for 14 consecutive days for it to work. It's perfectly okay to take a day off (or longer) whenever you need, but it is important to do the days in the order we present them. Each day's insights and practices build on the preceding ones, so to get the most out of the book, be sure to do Days 1–14 sequentially.

After, in part 3, we'll give you the tools to create a working template going forward and cement what you've done during the boot camp into lifelong habits.

Life can, indeed, be stressful. But within all its messy complexity are also the joys, empowering challenges, and rewards that make being human the rich experience that it is. We don't want you to miss out on one more minute of it because of stress. With these tools, you will be able to ride the ups and downs with grace, and to cultivate the unshakable inner confidence that comes from knowing you can deftly handle whatever comes your way.

PART

ONE
Missing Peace

1

One Nation, Under Stress

Meet Heather, forty-six. Heather is a working mom, married with two kids, ages fourteen and nine. If you took a quick, superficial look at Heather, you'd think she has it all together. She's good at her marketing job. She seems competent and in control. She's happy in her marriage, her kids are healthy, well-adjusted, and excelling in school. She has close friends with whom she occasionally grabs coffee (or something a little stronger). It's a good life.

But if you were to scratch the surface just a bit and take a closer look, you'd see that Heather is that proverbial duck on a pond. Above the water, it appears that she's gliding effortlessly. But just below, her legs are paddling awfully hard just to stay in place. At work there's the constant push to produce more results with fewer resources, which almost every day nudges Heather from chilling to simmering on the stress scale. There are the two jobs she has been doing for the past eighteen months: her own and the job of the guy who was downsized and never replaced, whose workload didn't just disappear along with him. So now Heather's plate is full to overflowing.

Then there's Heather the Mom, with her role as activities director and limo driver to her kids. Their endless cycle of doctor appointments, science fairs, and soccer tournaments often conflicts with important commitments Heather has at work, and she feels guilty and torn, always fearful of letting down either her boss or her family. Add in a broken car transmission, financial worries, and concerns about her aging mother who continually falls but refuses to move to an assisted-living facility, and Heather can easily find herself in the freak-out zone once, twice, three times or more a week.

Heather wistfully recalls how she used to play tennis as a way to blow off steam—something she hasn't done in months. And forget about what used to be a fulfilling social life. She recently discovered an invitation to an old friend's long-past wedding in a pile that she never even opened, let alone responded to. Her weight is creeping up as the number of hours she sleeps each night goes down. She comes home most days exhausted and irritable, and though she doesn't mean to, she takes it out on her husband, sparking arguments that seem to have no possible resolution.

Sure, Heather knows exercise would help, but that would mean taking time away from her family, which she doesn't want to do. Of course, working less would be ideal, but that's not an option, either. Heather is all too aware that her stress is damaging her health, her relationships, and her quality of life, but she can't see the way out. She has just accepted that this is the way things are.

Sound familiar?

We're guessing you have your own version of Heather's story. And you're not alone—far from it. Stress is quickly becoming a modern-day epidemic. High-powered or unemployed, married or single, we're a culture of seriously stressed people. According to a poll taken by the American Psychological Association in 2010, 75 percent of us reported feeling overloaded and stretched to the max in every direction. Think about that: three-quarters of the population said they felt they were *at their limit of capacity*. It hasn't gotten any better since: in 2012, 73 percent of us reported our stress had either stayed the same or gotten worse. That's a lot of people out there who are living in a constant state of overwhelm and anxiety.

The Stress Fallout

Is stress really so bad? Well, yes and no. In and of itself, stress is a normal biological response to overwhelming or threatening situations; it helps us through the high-pressure stuff of life. Our brilliant brain wiring has provided the fight-or-flight mechanism that gives us the boost we need in extreme circumstances.

But *chronic* stress is another story.

Our human stress system developed at least four hundred thousand years ago to deal with acute threats, like running away from a lion. Without that necessary response, you wouldn't have the reflexes or speed, and you'd be lunch. But now, that same stress system is being asked to cope with low-grade, persistent stressors like fear of downsizing, shuttling our kids from one activity to the next, rarely getting quality alone time with our spouse, being on call 24/7, a shrinking 401(k), and aging parents. Stressors like these are not your average "fight-or-flight" situations. Daily, we get that spike of adrenaline, again and again, without getting the peaceful downtime after the crisis has passed.

Chronic elevated stress levels wear down your body and your brain. It's much like flooring the gas pedal with your car in park. Do it for a prolonged period and something in your engine will break. Our bodies were not designed to process the constant influx of information and competing demands of twenty-first-century life any more than they are built to digest a constant intake of food, and indeed, we are breaking down at an alarming rate.

According to the American Academy of Family Physicians, two out of three office visits are for stress-related symptoms. Stress elevates our risk for serious illness, including heart disease and certain cancers. It's no joke, this stress business. Simply put, living our modern lifestyle with our caveman stress system is killing us.

We could talk a lot about what chronic stress does to your mind, body, and life, but chances are, if you're reading this book, you're already living it. You know firsthand how stress impairs your focus, saps your energy, and jeopardizes your health and your relationships. We're not going to spend pages detailing the evils of this phenomenon; you don't need us to convince you that stress is getting in the way of your enjoyment of life. That's why you're here to begin with.

If you're anything like the thousands of people we've worked with who are anxious, depressed, and frustrated by how they feel on a daily basis, you just want to feel better. And *fast*. You want to stop feeling pulled in ten different directions at once and regain a sense of control over your life. You want the calm and confidence that comes from knowing you are equipped to handle whatever comes your way. You want to know the way out of the stress maze so that you can stop coping and start living.

That's what we're here for.

2

A New Approach

Chances are, you didn't just wake up one day to find your life and well-being spinning out of control. And chances are, too, that you've sought out and made a real go of other methods for regaining balance and feeling more engaged and fulfilled.

So why are you here, reading yet another book? Why are you still seeking a solution?

The answer to that is that traditional stress-reduction methods only provide temporary relief. These methods don't last because they take a singular approach. Relaxation is great, and even healthy, but it's a one-note song. It won't eliminate your stress any more than declining one piece of pie after dinner made anyone thin.

Meditation, biofeedback, breathing exercises, going fishing or for a run: all of these things are useful to decompress, but they are not a permanent fix. They address the symptom, not the root cause, so their effects are fleeting. A massage might feel wonderful physically, for instance, and even soothe your mind, but the calm you've enjoyed vaporizes as soon as an e-mail from a disgruntled client or coworker hits your in-box.

Stress is not a simple cause-and-effect equation; it's brought about (and magnified or minimized) by a constellation of factors. Just as with any lifestyle change, we need a multidimensional approach to manage it better. Our goal in creating meQuilibrium was to create a whole-life approach to fix the problem from the inside out—for good. Not by eradicating your stress but by teaching you the secrets for living with it in balance.

That's what makes this program different from anything you've tried before. By merging our combined expertise and research, we created an empirically validated system that will hit your stress matrix from every angle, dissolving its hold on you.

The meQuilibrium Story

In 2009, Jan Bruce was at the helm of the leading wellness publication in the country. An accomplished media entrepreneur with an established track record in identifying emerging health trends, she was at the height of her career, in a glamorous, high-profile position that many would have envied. All this, plus a loving husband and two children at home—it would have been easy to assume Jan had it all.

Yet despite the successes, Jan felt fried. Just like Heather, whom you met earlier, she was on 24/7 with little to no respite, and things began to spin out of control. She wasn't the only one. Surrounded by the brightest and most successful executives in media and in the largest companies in the health and wellness industries, Jan saw how they—people who had the knowledge and resources needed to incorporate good diet, fitness, downtime, work/life balance, and rejuvenation into their lives—were also struggling to make these things happen. Everywhere she looked, smart, savvy people were frustrated, overwhelmed, and burned out.

Jan was an expert on wellness and healthy living, yet she still couldn't seem to fix the problem in her own life. That's when she saw what was missing. If someone as tapped into cutting-edge wellness as she was couldn't find balance, she knew we needed a better solution.

One day, Jan and a trusted colleague were talking about the latest health trends and they got it. According to the Centers for Disease Control, $847 billion is spent annually on stress, and 60 percent of all health care costs are attributable to preventable, lifestyle-related diseases like obesity. With her trademark instincts, Jan pinpointed stress as the next frontier in healthy lifestyle management. Like exercise and nutrition in decades past, it was time for stress to come out of the shadows. Too many people were craving balance, without any sustainable, proven resource to get them there. She realized it was time to create a lifestyle approach to managing stress—not just another fad "diet" but an accessible, practical, whole-life system to help people take control of their busy lives and regain their balance.

Jan set out to assemble the top minds to tackle this problem. Her first stop was Dr. Andrew Shatté, renowned psychologist and research professor in the College of Medicine at the University of Arizona and Brookings Institution fellow. Author of *The Resilience Factor*, Andrew is the foremost expert on the topic of

> "Stress is the new fat. It makes us sick, depletes us emotionally, and diminishes our quality of life."
>
> —Jan

resilience. He has spent more than twenty years researching resilience and developing skills to boost it, and has established resilience programs that are operating around the world. Andrew's work had shown that resilience is a foundational skill that can have powerful effects in many settings, including preventing depression in children at risk, helping young adults overcome setbacks as they enter college life, and improving productivity and performance at organizations ranging from NASA to Fortune 100 companies. Given those dramatic results, Jan and Andrew realized that resilience was the obvious antidote to stress.

Andrew had an unrivaled track record in helping people build this critical skill. What we feel and do in response to adversity (our resilience) is dictated by our habitual thoughts—what Andrew calls our *thinking styles*. We build resilience by changing how we think. Andrew isolated the core thinking styles that impact stress and developed concrete, proven tools for changing how we respond in the face of challenges.

That gave the program the chops to help people remedy the bad (i.e., stress), which was great. But Andrew knew from his work in positive psychology that in order to make it stick, we also needed to dial into the positive. We forge resilience by changing how we think, and we cement it by adding natural stress buffers, like experiencing the positive emotions—happiness, contentment, pride, and joy—and a sense of meaning and purpose in work and in life. The breakthrough skills he created to clean up the bad and root you firmly in the good—many of

> "The single most important place to start getting leverage on our stress isn't in what we do—it's in how we think."
> —Andrew

which you'll read about in this book—formed the basis of the meQuilibrium program.

Between Jan and Andrew, we had the mind skills and real-life application covered, but there was still more. Stress has tentacles in every area of our lives: our minds, our daily lives, and, of course, our bodies. We knew we needed someone with expertise in tackling that kind of interconnected web, and who better than one of the nation's foremost integrative medicine physicians? That's when we connected with Dr. Adam Perlman, executive director of Duke Integrative Medicine and one of the leading voices in revolutionizing medical care. Adam's medical expertise provided the essential skills to hit the biggest manifestations of stress in the body (think insomnia or overeating), and his clinical and experiential knowledge of the powerful mind/body/lifestyle connection helped us tie the whole program together.

As Adam explains, so much impacts our health and overall quality of life: what we do and eat, whether we move (or not), our relationships, as well as our sense of meaning and purpose. In traditional medicine, we tend to think only of physical health. But what about things like environment? Relationships? Spirituality? Or even your life's mission? Integrative medicine looks at the whole person and how the individual elements of life work together to impair or optimize mental and physical well-being.

It's much the same with stress. Stress has causes and consequences in our minds, emotions, physical health, lifestyle habits,

> "The root of the word *health* doesn't mean *to cure*. It means *to make whole*. That philosophy is at the heart of integrative medicine, and of our approach."
>
> —Adam

and surroundings. Just as all these factors come together in a complex web to make you *you*, they also comprise your stress. They're all connected, and each impacts the other. It's hard to think clearly or regulate your emotions, for instance, if you're not sleeping well. If you're not thinking clearly, you're probably getting backed up at work and overwhelmed by seemingly unsolvable problems . . . which leads to more stress. It's all connected.

To tackle stress, we need to hit it from every angle, and that's what we've done with this program. Through our combined expertise and extensive research, we isolated the twenty-four core factors that impact stress (some of which create it, some of which magnify it, and some of which relieve or act as a buffer against it) and created a practical system that transforms every facet. Our program has profoundly changed the lives of thousands of people. And now it's your turn.

Stress is not a badge of honor. Feeling overwhelmed is not an inevitable state of being that we need to grit our teeth and suffer through. While we can't banish stress entirely, it is something we can manage, and it's time to learn exactly how to live with it.

Just like managing your weight, managing your stress is about becoming aware of your choices and making better ones, and rewiring your thinking so that your habits sustain rather than sabotage your well-being. It's about creating a lifestyle that engages your mind, body, and support systems so that true balance becomes an integrated and ingrained way of life.

What makes this program different from anything you've tried before is that it doesn't teach you how to just alleviate stress. It shows you how to go farther upstream to address the root causes and create a sustainable center of calm. Then you can take on the challenges and stressors of life with grace. This is a total body-and-mind, inside-and-out approach to getting lasting relief.

The Payoff

Let's get to what's really important here: you. What are you going to get out of all of this? Here's the takeaway you'll get by investing 15 to 30 minutes each day for the next 14 days:

TACKLE YOUR THINKING STYLES

Your resilience determines your ability to stay afloat, which in turn determines your stress levels and quality of life. So what determines who is resilient and who is not? What makes one person bounce back from adversity and another crumble?

The answer to that is *thinking styles*. One of the most important ingredients in resilience is controlling your emotions and behaviors, and that means controlling your thoughts. As we shall see, how we think has a profound influence on our ability to handle stress. If we want all the good stuff that resilience produces, and better stress management, then we've got to tackle our thinking styles.

Thinking styles are the familiar ways in which we see the world and our place in it. They dictate how we view ourselves, our circumstances, our future— even how we believe the world or we *should be*.

> "More than education, more than experience, it is resilience that determines who succeeds and who fails, who is satisfied in their jobs and in their relationships, who is physically and emotionally healthy, and who is happy."
>
> —Andrew

The problem is, we develop habits around how we think. We do this because it's time effective, but it's inefficient because our thinking habits are often wrong. One of the reasons we have such difficulty with work/life conflict is because we're bringing the same old tired thinking habits to the table each day.

That's what's different here. We get your head in the game. We'll show you clearly how what you think can have a profound effect on what you feel and do. You'll learn to think differently so that you can become more accurate in your assessments of situations, recognize problematic thinking styles, and learn how to navigate around them to effect change.

With this program, you will learn how to:

- Identify your habitual thinking traps
- Zap the thoughts that cloud your problem-solving abilities
- Free yourself from unwarranted negative emotions that bog you down
- Reclaim control of how you respond to life's challenges
- Take back your time
- Achieve work/life balance
- Maintain calm under pressure
- Regain your clarity and focus

The result: You'll become far more empowered and better equipped to pull yourself out of stress messes, and able to more fluidly flow through the ups and downs of your everyday life.

REMOVE THE ROADBLOCKS TO HEALTHY LIVING

You're smart. You intuitively know that your body is significantly better equipped to stave off stress if it is fueled with the right foods, if your mood and energy are boosted by exercise, and if you get restorative rest and good sleep. You've likely looked at a lot of tools for better living, including diet, exercise, and time management, and we know you're sincerely trying to live the best and most balanced life you can. We know you want a saner, calmer, healthier life for yourself, so really, why isn't it happening?

We'll give you two good reasons. The first is that stress is the ultimate catch-22. The more stressed you are, the less able you are to make the changes that would alleviate it. Stress saps our energy and motivation, leaving us too drained to care for ourselves so that we can stay ahead of it. Think about it: How motivated are you to cook a healthy meal or work out when you're exhausted? When you're troubled at work, how likely are you to seek out joyful ways to revive your spirits? If you're overwhelmed by your to-do list, how likely are you to snooze peacefully to refresh your mind so that you can get ahead of tomorrow's list?

The second reason runs a little deeper: faulty thinking. Whenever we engage in behavior that seems self-sabotaging or absurd, there's always a reason for it. There are forces (aka thinking styles) keeping your behaviors in place, and we'll show you how to unearth those forces so that they don't have you repeating the same patterns of behavior.

If you've tried to make changes in these areas before and have not succeeded, it's because you've tried to change at the behavioral level, rather than trying to change the underlying thoughts pushing those behaviors. If they're to stick, lifestyle changes cannot be made on the surface level. If you don't go farther upstream and address how you think, you really *can't* change. It's not possible. Even if you get a little traction, it's not permanent, because the same old thinking traps and mistakes you've made in the past will override these behavior changes. It's not a failure of willpower; you're simply falling into some basic traps in terms of how you see the world that are tripping you up.

> "Ideally, you don't want to wait until you are faced with a health crisis to start making lifestyle changes for managing stress. That's like learning to use a nail gun the day you need to build a house."
>
> —Adam

We aren't going to insult you by simply pushing another diet, exercise, or time-management plan in your direction. Instead, we will equip you with the essential skills you've been missing out on to make these things happen.

You will learn how to:

- Identify and get control of the thinking styles and triggers that have derailed your healthy efforts in the past
- Sleep better, longer, and more soundly
- Take the stress out of exercise
- Easily gain control of your eating habits

We'll get you out of feeling too busy, too stuck, too exhausted, or just too darn stressed to do anything about your physical health and into feeling energized, motivated, and equipped with proven strategies to make your new wellness habits stick.

BOLSTER YOUR NATURAL STRESS BUFFERS

Having a sense of meaning and purpose . . . joy and laughter . . . supportive relationships . . . a deep connection to something greater than yourself—these positive experiences do more than just make us feel good. Just like exercise, healthy eating, and sound sleep, they are all natural buffers against stress.

If you're stressed, the last thing you want to hear is that you need to feel more fulfilled or to inject a sense of meaning and purpose into your life. Please. You're just looking to cope! And we'll get you there. But to *keep* you there, we need to lead you into the realm of the positive.

This program goes well beyond stress management. It's a whole-life system for creating sustained contentment and balance. We know you want to live a full, happy life; you're just hitting impediments. We're going to help you remove those impediments and give you concrete skills for getting to the good stuff. (For all of you who are reading this thinking, "I don't have the time to fit in anything good," we're asking you to take a leap of faith. By the end of the program, you'll have mastered skills that will afford you much more time to enjoy your life than perhaps you can now imagine.)

> "The opposite of stress isn't happiness. It's not being fulfilled or inspired. It's just . . . not stressed. Even if you could eradicate stress, fixing what's broken can only get you to zero. But really, who wants to live their life at zero? We want to—and can—dial our lives well into the positive."
>
> —Andrew

Over the next 14 days, you will learn concrete skills to:

- Banish burnout
- Tip the balance of good and bad events in your daily life in your favor (the more good you have stacked up, the less impacted you are by the bad)
- Reenergize your work
- Identify your deeper purpose and take easy steps to align your actions with your goals
- Tap the deep wellspring of resilience that comes from connecting to something greater that yourself
- Reinfuse your life with satisfaction and joy

ACHIEVE "meQuilibrium"

This, after all, is why you're really here.

meQuilibrium is more than just a program. It's a state of mind. At the end of these two weeks, you'll find that state of bliss, enjoyment, balance, and vitality that we know you're looking for. No more feeling overwhelmed, anxious, or adrift. No more striving to be just "not stressed" or experiencing temporary relief. It's past time to find the sustainable calm you're seeking and peacefully enjoy this life of yours to the fullest.

PART

TWO

The 14-Day Reboot

3

14 Days to meQuilibrium

We've distilled our program into 14 essential skills that will put you back in control of your life. The flow of these skills is scientifically designed to get the needle to move on your stress radar instantly--and then cumulatively. We've seen improvement for our clients in as little as one day. We've front-loaded this program to give you the maximum benefit as quickly as possible in order to motivate you to keep going.

The 14-Day Reboot is very simple to follow. All you need to do is commit 15 to 30 minutes per day. That's all: 15 to 30 minutes daily for 14 days to completely turn your life around. It's a small investment of time for a very significant payoff. Each day, we'll take you through one of the key skills, giving you exact instructions for how to put it to immediate use in your everyday life. Read the material and follow our cues to write your daily plan for implementing the skill. Really, that's it. We've done the rest.

Good habits are easier to make and keep when you believe you're worth it. You deserve to be a top priority. We all have big

"You can never get today back. The small events that you worry about end up having so little impact on you long-term. How much of your life have you given up to being anxious about them? Or the bigger question: How many hours and days do you have left, and how do you want to spend them?"

—Adam

ideas of how we'd like our lives to be. But putting new habits in place and replacing bad ones is where the rubber meets the road. While it isn't easy, there are few things that can change your life more dramatically than learning to manage your stress. You just have to believe your life is worth it.

Because it is.

Day One

Calm Your Emotions

The Payoff: Freedom from debilitating emotions and a deeper reserve of composure and clarity

Stress, as we know it, is a feeling. When we're in the positive zone of happiness, pride, fulfillment, and the like, life feels pretty good. We're in control and content. But when we get sucked into a vortex of negative emotions, like anxiety, anger, frustration, sadness, and guilt, we not only feel bad—we get a double whammy because those emotions cloud our thinking and prevent us from effectively solving the problems we're facing. If you've ever felt too anxious or too frustrated to think clearly or handle a situation calmly, you know what we're talking about.

> "We may not be able to solve whatever is going on with your kids, or at work, but we can help you get the emotion regulation you need to handle those situations effectively. You'll be calmer and more in control."
>
> —Andrew

The skill of emotion regulation comes first, on Day 1, because getting control of your emotions is the single most critical component of stress management. It ranks number one on our list of twenty-four factors that impact one's overall stress profile. We're going to teach you a powerful tool for getting rid of your negative, unwarranted, and undeserved emotions. You can literally change your life with just this one simple skill.

Emotions are a natural part of human existence. But powerful surges of negative emotions can be all-consuming and impede our ability to function, which makes stressful events even more stressful. The goal is not to eradicate these emotions; to some degree, they serve us by protecting or motivating us. We wouldn't get off the sofa if we didn't experience some anxiety. Instead, we're looking to neutralize powerful emotions *when they are not warranted*. They suck up our problem-solving energy, wasting precious resources on phantom problems and not leaving enough for the ones that legitimately merit our best thinking. Our goal is for you to lose not one minute more to a negative emotion that is not real and justified.

Emotion regulation—the ability to keep your runaway negative emotions in check and remain goal-focused—is the cornerstone of resilience, which, as you know, is the antidote to stress. So, you can understand why emotion regulation is key.

Ready, Set, Steady

So, how do we get to the even ground of emotion regulation? By tuning in to and challenging the thoughts that dictate our feelings. Every emotion we feel is caused by a thought. For instance, a thought about a future threat produces anxiety (e.g., "I could get fired"). A thought about violation produces anger

("That was my parking spot!"). Thoughts of loss trigger sadness ("He doesn't love me anymore"). Thoughts of not meeting your own standards generate shame ("I didn't do what I said I was going to do"). On a daily basis, these can be some of

> **THOUGHT FEED**: The stream of thoughts that run constantly through your mind, like background noise, that unconsciously dictates your emotions.

the hundreds of thoughts that run endlessly through our minds, much like the constant news stream on our television screens. We've become so accustomed to this information feed that we hardly notice it, but it's there all the same. We call these streaming thoughts your *thought feed*.

These thought feeds arise as a direct result of what Andrew refers to as our *emotion radar*. Just as we develop habits in what we wear and how we talk, we develop habits in how we think. Some of us automatically scan our worlds for a future threat (creating anxiety), some scan

> **EMOTION RADAR**: Our habitual way of scanning for clues about what's happening to and around us in the world.

for a violation of their rights (generating anger), and others might scan for how they violated the rights of another (the hallmark thought behind guilt). These scanning tendencies *are* your emotion radar.

This radar is your way of perceiving the world and how your brain searches for clues about what's happening out there. The problem is that your radar only scans within a very limited range. If you have an anger-tuned radar, for instance, it's scanning for opportunities to light up with a "Ka-ching! My rights have been violated!" A sadness radar scans the world for what you've lost or are missing out on. When your radar pings on something, your emotions get triggered.

The problem is that your emotion radar may be so strong and automatic that it causes you to feel emotions that are not warranted, and these emotions exacerbate our stress. They obscure our thinking and our ability to problem-solve, which further gets in the way when we're trying to find our way through pressure-packed situations. Certainly, there are times that we legitimately feel angry or anxious or sad, but today we're looking at the proportion of times that we get unnecessarily overpowered by these emotions. If we're not aware of it, our emotion radar can run the show and cause us to feel troubling emotions without prompting us to pause and see if they're truly warranted.

Again, if you've ever felt too angry, too anxious, too *anything* to deal with a situation calmly, you know what we mean. We've all been there. The good news is that we can show you the way out.

The 7 Big Emotions

There are seven primary negative emotions that have the ability to ramp up our stress levels: anger, anxiety, frustration, sadness, guilt, embarrassment, and shame. We can feel a mix of emotions at any one time, but ninety-nine out of one hundred people can easily pinpoint the emotion that most gets in their way. What emotion do you go to first when you're experiencing something bad? Is it anxiety? Anger? That's your default emotion. It's the one that your radar is tuned in to above all others, so it scans for it, looking for any and all opportunities to light up your emotional screen and wreak havoc on your equilibrium.

THE SOURCE OF EMOTION RADARS: What makes one person scan for loss while another scans for a violation of his or her rights? No surprise, we inherit our thinking habits of emotion radars from our parents and the formative environment in which we were raised. For instance, if you grew up with a dad who was always looking for who was going to screw him over next, you might inherit that tendency to scan for a violation of your rights. If your parents were highly overprotective, you might absorb their belief that the world is a dangerous place and learn to scan for a future threat.

Fortunately, we don't have to live at the mercy of our emotion radars. Once we become aware of them and learn the tools for unhooking from the emotions, we take back our control—and our serenity.

• •

Most people go through life believing that it's the situation we're in that determines what we feel. But that's not really the case. If it were, then each and every one of us would react the same in any given situation, and of course, we don't. There's an important variable in there, and that is *what we think* about the situation in which we find ourselves.

Take, for example, encountering a long line at the DMV. If you're dialed in to frustration, you might walk in, see the line, and immediately focus on the fact that you have no control over your position in line or the speed at which it moves. With anger, you would focus on the violation of your right to good service. With sadness, you may flash on what you're missing out on by being in this line, like precious time with your family. In each of these scenarios, that's your emotion radar at work.

Everything that happens to us is filtered through our belief systems. Behind every feeling is a belief, and that belief colors what we see and how we respond. In other words, the feeling may not be a direct result of what is actually happening but of what we *believe* is happening. Challenge the belief and you have the opportunity to assess clearly the merits of that feeling.

Let's put this to a real-life test.

Imagine that you've been working very long hours for the past several weeks to complete a crucial project. Night after night, you've been burning the midnight oil. After many weeks of this, you come home after a particularly tough day, particularly late, and as you walk through the front door of your home, you realize immediately that the atmosphere is frosty. All is not well. You're confronted at the door by your spouse or significant other, who says, "You know what, I'm sick of this. You're a workaholic, and you simply don't make our relationship a priority."

In that moment, what thoughts would run through your mind? What would you feel and do?

THE ANGER RADAR

Anger is a very normal response here. Your face flushes, your muscles tense, and your heart starts pounding. Your thought feed would probably go something like this: *"I don't believe this. I'm not doing this job for my health. We agreed on a lifestyle, a couple of kids, a mortgage, and two cars. To fund that lifestyle, I need to keep this job. Frankly, I could do with a little more support from you right now."*

As you now know, the anger thought feed is all about feeling a violation of your rights—in this particular case, the right to have support from your partner in a time of need. For some, this is not a one-off. Since childhood, you may have been operating with a built-in radar that scans your world for violation: *Who's taking advantage of me? How and where am I getting cheated?* The reality is that if you scan hard enough for something, you'll find it, even if it's not there or is misdirected. To quote Aristotle, "Anybody can become angry—that is easy. But to be angry with the right person and to the right degree and at the right time and for the right purpose, and in the right way—that is not within everybody's power and is not easy."

> **ANGER FACT:** Getting angry causes stress not just in your head but also in your heart. According to a study published in the *Journal of the American College of Cardiology,* anger sets off electrical impulses in the heart that can increase the likelihood of arrhythmias. Other studies have shown that patients who have heart attacks most frequently report being angry right before the event.

THE ANXIETY RADAR

How many of you would feel at least a little anxious if your significant other confronted you with that same workaholic accusation? Anxiety produces butterflies in the stomach, tingling fingers, cold feet, a dry mouth, and rapid heartbeat. Your thought feed looks something like: *"This isn't good. Something's got to give here. Either my career or relationship is going to suffer."*

The thoughts that fuel anxiety are all about the fear of a perceived future threat. Just as with violation for those with an anger radar, look hard enough for danger coming down the road and you'll find it, even if it's not really there. Mark Twain wrote, "I've lived through many terrible things in my life, some of which actually happened."

THE FRUSTRATION RADAR

Perhaps instead of (or in addition to) feeling angry, you feel frustrated by this encounter. Again, that's a normal response. Frustration is a physical hybrid, mixing the agitation of anxiety with the flush of anger.

Your thoughts might run to something like: "*There's nothing I can do here. I have no options. I'd rather be at home more but I can't; I've got to be at work.*" It's the classic feeling of being stuck between a rock and a hard place. If this is your common radar pattern, it falls into the bucket of beliefs known as lack of resources. For some people, this isn't a one-off. Their radar is tuned to pick up on the resources they don't have rather than the ones that they do. This radar will lead them to see all the things they don't have as larger-than-life, while the things they do have appear to be microscopic.

THE SADNESS RADAR

Sadness shows up in our bodies like a heavy weight bearing down; some describe the sensation of moving very slowly, as if through molasses. It also often brings with it the feeling of being on the verge of tears.

Your sadness thought feed for the same scenario would show as something like this: "*I thought our relationship was better than this. I thought we had an understanding and were in sync about my work.*" The fundamental belief behind those deeply attuned to sadness is that they've lost something. Perhaps it's a real-world loss, like losing a job, a relationship, or even your wallet. Or maybe it's a loss of self-esteem or a sense of self-worth, when you thought you were good at something and suddenly realize you're not, as in, "I thought I was really strong in that interview, but not getting the job shows me I wasn't." Or perhaps it's what psychologists refer to as the ideal/real gap, as in, "I thought my relationship was way up there, but I just got a sudden reminder that it's down here." The bigger the gap between the ideal and the real, the greater the sadness.

THE UPSIDE TO DOWN EMOTIONS: Emotions are a biological and evolutionary gift. For instance, when we're sad or grieving, we slow down. Thousands of years ago, that would have meant we'd get eaten by a predator. So sadness also comes with a hardwired drive to withdraw, keeping us inside (in caves or otherwise) and safe until our strength and full faculties return. There are similarly good reasons for the other emotions, as well, such as anxiety in the face of danger to activate our fight-or-flight response, or guilt as a marker that we've stepped on someone's toes and need to mend that fence (a valuable signal for a socially interdependent species like us). So you see, we're not looking to eradicate our seven big emotions; just zap them when they're not warranted.

- -

THE GUILT RADAR

Those of you for whom guilt is the default emotion know its sting all too well. Guilt combines the agitation of anxiety with the heavy weight of sadness. The guilt radar is tuned to scan for how and when you've violated the rights of others. Continuing our imagined homecoming scenario, your guilt thought feed would go something like this: "*You know what, he or she is right. My family deserves better, and I'm letting them down. I should be spending more time at home.*"

THE EMBARRASSMENT RADAR

Besides agitation, the giveaway that embarrassment is kicking in is a feeling of wanting to get away from the situation as fast as possible. Those with a highly tuned embarrassment radar scan for situations in which they've lost standing in someone's eyes. They might think something like this: "*I thought I was doing so well keeping all these balls in the air, but they're dropping and he/she can see I'm not managing well.*"

EMOTION RADARS

PHYSICAL SENSATION	EMOTION	THOUGHT FEED
Flushed or hot face, clenched fists or teeth, rapid heartbeat	Anger	"My rights have been violated."
Rapid heartbeat, tense muscles, dry mouth, butterflies in your stomach, lightheadedness	Anxiety	"Something bad is going to happen."
Red flush of anger mixed with the fidgety restlessness of anxiety	Frustration	"I don't have the resources I need."
Feeling of a heavy weight bearing down on you, moving slowly, feeling on the verge of tears	Sadness	"I've lost something."
Agitation of anxiety mixed with the heavy weight of sadness	Guilt	"I've violated someone else's rights."
Restless, agitated, reddened face, strong desire to get away from the situation, feeling like others are looking at or judging you	Embarrassment	"I've lost standing in someone's eyes."
Hollow feeling in the pit of the stomach, nagging sense that you've done something wrong, bowing your head or avoiding eye contact	Shame	"I've broken my own standards."

THE SHAME RADAR

Shame shows up as a hollow sensation in the pit of your stomach or a nagging sense that you've done something wrong. Those who feel shame tend to bow their heads and avert their eyes. A person who responds with shame in this scenario would have a thought feed that whispers something like this: *"I know people should put family first, and I'm disappointed in myself."* If we take a look at the bucket of beliefs behind shame, we see that it's about breaking our own rules of how we believe we should live in the world.

Take Action

To get control of your emotions, you're going to use a skill that we call Trap It, Map It, Zap It (TMZ for short). This is a key skill in the program to get in touch with what's really driving you off the cliff cognitively and emotionally. It will help you analyze what's going on in any high-stress situation and assess whether your reaction is accurate or whether it's just a habitual response that's exacerbating the situation. The trick is to understand what you're feeling and thinking to see if it's helping or hurting you in that moment. Then you can respond accordingly from a place of calm, with a cool head and clear thinking. This method will show up quite a few times throughout the program in different ways. It's very potent and surprisingly easy to employ.

Whenever a strong surge of negative emotion threatens to derail you, follow these three steps:

1. Trap It. Early detection is key. What are you feeling exactly? Use your physical sensations to identify the emotion as soon as you feel one coming on, using the Emotion Radars chart on page 32. We're better at detecting our feelings than our thoughts, so although thoughts produce emotions, we have to look downstream at how we're feeling to get a handle on our thinking. We need to become very aware of what our pet emotions feel like in mind,

body, and behavior so that as soon as they begin, we can trap them.

2. Map It. To find the thought, connect the feeling to the thought that is causing it (until you can quickly do so on your own, you can use the Emotion Radars chart on page 32). For instance, "I'm getting angry right now, so where am I detecting my rights being violated?" Try to be as precise about the violation thought as possible.

3. Zap It. Here's where you'll challenge the thought. Ask yourself, is this feeling warranted, or is it my emotional radar pinging on something that isn't really there? Each thought feed has a corresponding thought zapper to help you decipher what's truly happening.

Nine times out of ten, you'll discover that the thought has no validity and it disappears, and the negative emotion right along with it. Do this enough times and the challenge becomes as automatic as it once was to become angry or sad or guilty. You've slowed down the mechanism enough to spot the faulty thinking, neutralize the negative emotion, and restore your ability to think clearly and problem-solve effectively.

Take meQuilibrium member Eric, age forty-eight. Eric is an anger guy; that's his default emotion in stressful situations. Eric travels frequently for business. On a recent trip to Chicago, he could hear the television set in the adjoining hotel room loud and clear. Annoyed because the television was distracting him from getting work done, Eric called downstairs to request a room change but was politely told the hotel was all booked. In the past, Eric might have stormed down to the front desk and demanded to speak to the manager, huffing and puffing until he either got his way . . . or didn't. In other words,

EMOTION	THOUGHT FEED	THOUGHT ZAPPER
Anger	"My rights have been violated."	"Have my rights truly been violated? Have I been cheated out of something I'm honestly entitled to?"
Anxiety	"Something bad is going to happen."	"What is the bad thing I think is going to happen to me? Is this really likely to happen, or is it just my emotion radar pinging on something that isn't there?"
Frustration	"I don't have the resources I need."	"What's the one thing I have in my toolbox—however small—that I can use to gain some leverage on this problem?"
Sadness	"I've lost something."	"Have I really lost this thing/person?"
Guilt	"I've violated someone else's rights."	"What do I think I owed this person, and would I expect them to give the same thing to me? If not, why the double standard?"
Embarrassment	"I've lost standing in someone's eyes."	"Other people are more concerned about their own image than they are about mine" and/or "Other people can't see what's going on for me internally."
Shame	"I've broken my own standards."	"What do I expect from myself? Is it a realistic, human-capacity standard I've set for myself here? Do I believe others have to live up to these standards?"

making a stressful situation even more stressful for himself. Instead, he employed the skill of TMZ. He:

1. Identified his familiar anger signals (clenched teeth and a strong desire to start barking and yelling at the responsible party).

2. Mapped the feeling to the violation-of-rights thought, which in this case went something like, "What is wrong with this guy? He's preventing me from getting my work done!"

3. Zapped the thought. Eric asked himself, "Is this person really violating my rights? Am I really more entitled to quiet than he is to watch TV?" That zapped it; when you get to the place where you can see the incongruity between your reaction and the event at hand—maybe even laugh at yourself a little—you've let the air out of the emotion.

In a calm, composed state, Eric went downstairs and talked to the front desk manager. Even though the hotel was fully booked, the manager appreciated Eric's patience and worked a little magic to find an open, nonadjoining room to accommodate him—something that likely wouldn't have happened if Eric had roared and ranted at him. Behold the quiet power of calm.

By the way, just because you have a finely tuned violation-of-rights radar doesn't mean your rights are never violated. As we said, nine times out of ten they're probably not, but there is that one time in the ten. Even then, once you recognize that your anger (or whichever of the other Big 7 Emotions you experience) is justified, you can neutralize it and respond from a calmer place.

Say, for example, a cab driver takes you on an unnecessarily out-of-the-way route. Having the self-awareness to distinguish that, yes, you actually are being taken advantage of is phenomenally powerful, because it neutralizes the zing of the emotion. Now it's just a fact—the driver is looking to make an extra few bucks off you—rather than a feeling clouding your ability to deal with the situation at hand. Your anger may be real and justified, but it's not helping you in the situation; now you can put it aside and get to a calmer place. You take the charge out of it and can then address your violation of rights in a clearheaded way.

When it comes to stress, emotion regulation is its own reward. Even if you get to the point after employing Trap It, Map It, Zap It where you realize you're stuck with the problem, you're still in a better place because you've short-circuited the knee-jerk connection between thought and emotional reaction. Where before you might have felt defeated, now you'll view the situation from the more peaceful vantage point of acceptance. That's better for your mind, your body—and usually for your success rate in handling situations.

You're now equipped with the tools to break free of your unwarranted negative emotions. No more feeling too anxious, too angry, too sad . . . too *anything* to function at your best. It's time to release their power over you. With this skill, you'll be able to take back control of how you feel and how you respond.

Enjoy the calm!

My Plan for Emotion Regulation

I choose to work on the skill of emotion regulation because:

My default emotion in stressful situations is:

This emotion shows up on a physical level for me in these ways:

The thought feed that fuels that emotion is:

The thought zapper I will use to zap the emotion when it is not warranted is:

Day Two

Sleep Smart

The Payoff: Restored energy to do the things that allow you to relieve stress effectively

You might be wondering why something as basic as sleep comes this early in the program, but we have good reason. Let's face it: when you're exhausted, you have zero capacity to manage stress. All the factors that make up stress are interconnected, and as our research shows, sleep is pivotal for stamina, health, mental focus, and emotion regulation (think about how hard it is to control your emotions when you're exhausted). Sleep basically makes all the other skills of stress management attainable. So we'll go after good sleep here, on Day 2, to get your physiological foundation set.

Bad sleep is ubiquitous. Sixty-seven percent of Americans surveyed in a National Sleep Foundation poll said they regularly have trouble sleeping. More than three-quarters of the patients who come to see Adam struggle with sleep issues. In our meQuilibrium sampling, 38 percent of participants gave themselves the poorest rating possible on sleeping, reporting that they "always have trouble falling asleep and/or with waking up during the night." Only 10 percent of those polled rated their sleep at the best level.

The usual suspects of poor sleep are to blame: sugar, caffeine, overworking, and, of course, stress. In fact, as you're probably well aware, the last one provokes a vicious cycle: stress keeps you from sleeping, and lack of sleep keeps you stressed. According to the Anxiety and Depression Association of America, 75 percent of adults whose sleep is compromised by stress or anxiety say that their sleep problems, in turn, have increased their levels of stress and anxiety.

> **THE SLEEP/STRESS CYCLE:** If you don't sleep well, you can't think clearly. If you can't think clearly, you can't effectively problem-solve. If you can't problem-solve, you're vulnerable to tired thinking traps, which further cloud your mental function and exacerbate stress. In turn, this causes insomnia, and around you go.

The worst sleepers in the meQuilibrium pool were shown to be one and a half times as stressed as the best sleepers. Poor sleep hits us on every level. Mentally, it fries our thinking and impairs our problem-solving capabilities. Our emotional resilience and outlook are compromised, as well. Compared to good sleepers, poor sleepers are 36 percent less optimistic and almost twice as vulnerable to burnout.

On a physical level, not getting quality sleep has been linked to everything from depression to lowered libido to heart disease to diabetes—all of which only add to the already-stacked stress pile.

But enough about the toll poor sleep can take. How about we look at the positive effect that getting a good night's rest can have on you, instead? Studies show that good sleep can:

- Improve learning
- Increase your attention span

- Increase your decision-making ability
- Help you cope better with change
- Help repair your heart and blood vessels
- Help balance the hormones that regulate appetite
- Increase your productivity at work or in school
- Improve your sex life

When it comes to stress, good sleep has a profound effect. In our studies, good sleepers scored significantly better on twenty-seven out of the twenty-eight stress factors. Their ability to think clearly, regulate their emotions, break through relationship impasses, balance their work and home life, manage their time, eat better, tap into a sense of meaning and purpose in their life . . . all these benefits correlated to getting better z's.

> **HOW MUCH SLEEP IS ENOUGH?**: In general, eight hours of sleep each night is considered the ideal. But most people don't live in the ideal, and it varies from person to person. It's really more about getting to understand your body. How do you feel on the days that you get six hours of sleep? On the days you sleep late and get nine or ten? Do you feel refreshed when you wake up in the morning? Pay attention not just to how you feel when you wake up but throughout the day. Is your cognitive functioning sharp? Are you able to control and regulate your emotions? All these are clues that will enable you to zero in on the number of hours of sleep that are optimal for you.

So it's important to make sleeping smart—which means sleeping better and longer—a priority. Often, it takes only a few small changes in your routine. Let's fix the simple pieces and get leverage where we can: in your habits. Then you can have more energy and capacity to do the things that will allow you to relieve stress effectively. You can do all the work of emotion regulation, and all the other highly effective skills you'll learn in the next 12 days, but if you're still compromising good sleep, you're negating your efforts.

Your sleep schedule, bedtime habits, and lifestyle choices make an enormous difference in sleep patterns. Use the tips below to create a tailored sleeping plan. You don't need to tackle all of these at once. Just choose one or two that you feel will have the most impact for you and commit to putting them into practice—tonight!

Here is Dr. Adam's prescription for healthy sleep habits.

If You Have Difficulty Falling Asleep

DO:
- Set a regular bedtime. Go to bed at around the same time every night and wake up around the same time every morning. Routine tells your body when you should be asleep and when you should be awake.

- Fight after-dinner drowsiness. If you find yourself getting sleepy well before your bedtime, get up and do something: call a friend, fold the laundry, do the dishes.

- Make your bed a sleep-only zone. This means no TV, computer, or radio while you're trying to fall asleep. These activities stimulate your brain and body and make falling asleep that much harder.

- Make your bedroom sleep-friendly. Keep it dark and quiet. White-noise machines and blackout shades work wonders!

- Create a relaxing bedtime routine. Leave yourself at least half an hour to calm yourself and ready your body, mind, and spirit for a good night's sleep. Some things to consider for your routine:

▷ Take a warm bath, adding a few drops of a soothing essential oil such as lavender to the water. Warm water releases stressed-out muscles, and lavender relaxes the mind and body.

▷ Listen to soothing music. Just be sure to turn off the music when you're ready to go to sleep.

▷ Read a light book or magazine (though not in bed; bed should be reserved for sleep and sex).

▷ Do some gentle stretches or calming yoga.

▷ Practice relaxing breathing (see page 68 in Day 4 for tips on technique).

- Consider a sleep supplement. Magnesium glycinate (240 mg before bedtime), melatonin (3 to 5 mg before bedtime for adults or 0.3 mg for elderly people), or even Sleepytime tea can help relax you. Please consult with your health professional for advice on what's right for you.

- Find a mantra. Repeating a simple mantra—the same sound or phrase over and over again—will relax your restless mind, calm your heart rate, and eventually send you into slumber. As you say it, listen for the sound of the syllables in your head. Let the sentences run together over and over again as the pitch and tone lull you to sleep. Find one or more that work for you, jot them down on a piece of paper, and keep them on a bedside table. Here are some examples:

▷ "Sleep will come when it comes."

▷ "Sleep cannot be rushed."

▷ "None of my problems is so big that it can't wait until tomorrow."

▷ "Things always look better and brighter in the light of day."

▷ "I work hard and deserve my sleep."

▷ "My sleep is well earned."

▷ "Sleep is easy—babies can do it."

DON'T:

- **Engage in vigorous exercise at night.** Any workouts that get your heart rate up are best done in the morning or afternoon. In the evenings, stick with a more relaxing routine like yoga.

- **Drink caffeine.** Avoid coffee, soda, and other caffeinated drinks after midafternoon.

- **Keep thoughts in your head.** Before bed, download what's on your mind so that it's less likely to keep you awake. Start a bedtime journal, and write down everything you're thinking about. Getting your thoughts and worries into your journal will get them out of your head for the time being and clear your mind. If anxious thoughts continue to keep you awake after you've tried implementing these tips, no worries; on Day 4, you'll learn highly effective calming skills to redirect your attention and quiet the internal chaos.

SLEEP AND THOUGHTS: Yesterday, you learned about the power of thoughts to impact your emotions. No surprise, they can also impact your ability to change your habits—including sleep. Some people hold beliefs around this that get in their way, like "Sleep is an expendable resource" or "Successful people don't need a lot of sleep." As you go through the program, you'll learn tools for challenging those beliefs, but for now, it's helpful just to become aware of any beliefs that might be preventing you from fully utilizing today's skill.

If You Have Difficulty Staying Asleep

DO:

• Engage in mindful sleep. For those nights when you wake up in the middle of the night, be mindful of what you did right before bedtime, and look for the culprit. Did you eat something different? Did you watch a dramatic television show? Did you have a glass of wine or smoke a cigarette right before bed? All of those things can lead to an unsettled sleep.

• Practice mindful dreaming. If a dream wakes you, try to remember as much of the dream as you can as soon as you wake up. Try to place yourself immediately back in the dream—as if you're the star of a movie and you're calling yourself back to the set for the next scene. This can help you fall back to sleep.

DON'T:

• Look at the time (no matter how tempting it is). Staring at the clock is counterproductive. It will only keep you awake, worrying that you won't get enough sleep.

- Drink alcohol close to bedtime. While alcohol may help you fall asleep, it may also wake you up to go to the bathroom, drink water, and then go to the bathroom again.

- Overeat before bed. Doing so could lead to indigestion and an overall rocky night's sleep.

- Put on bright lights. If you have to get up in the middle of the night to get a drink or go to the bathroom, use only enough light so that you don't crash into anything. If you get up to read on an electronic device, use the nighttime setting or lower the brightness. Bright lights may bring you fully awake and make it more difficult to get back to sleep.

> **WHEN SLEEP PROBLEMS WON'T GO AWAY:** Sometimes difficulties with sleep are caused by hormonal shifts or a sleep disorder that should be treated by your physician. Always discuss your concerns about your sleep with your doctor, particularly if you are falling asleep spontaneously during the day, have been told you snore or seem to be gasping for air when you sleep, if you awaken yourself or your partner by kicking your arms or legs, or repeatedly suffer from a restless feeling in your body at night. If you awaken not feeling refreshed, a hormonal imbalance or a more significant sleep disorder might need the attention of a physician or sleep expert.

Making even one of these simple changes can yield big results. Start tonight, and within a few days, you're likely to see some pretty drastic improvement in how you feel and how you respond to stress. What do you have to lose other than your exhaustion?

My Plan for Sleeping Smart

I choose to work on this skill because:

The sleep-smart skills I will practice tonight are:

I will implement them in these specific ways:

Day Three

Unlock Your Problem-Solving Power

Q *The Payoff: Clear thinking and a keener ability to solve everyday problems*

Ask one hundred people what "stress" is and most will point to the mountain of unsolvable problems in their lives: the frustrating boss, the relationship standoff, the scheduling challenges that make it seem utterly impossible to fit in all the things we need and want to do. Today you're going to learn to bust through those bottlenecks that are causing you stress. It's time to unlock your problem-solving power with the most formidable tool you have at your disposal: your mind.

Life's complications can, without a doubt, be maddening. The reality, however, is that we can make our problems seem more insurmountable than they really are through habitual faulty thinking—our thinking styles. The problem, as you know, is that our thinking styles often don't serve us. Reverting to habits is easy, and when we're stressed, we seek easy. Ironically, these mental habits make things worse and more stressful. Just when we need to be thinking most clearly—when we're stressed—we fall into the familiar habits that most trip us up.

We can't solve all of life's problems or make them go away. But we can teach you how to more effectively solve them for yourself. Today we're going to share with you a signature mind skill to help you identify and recalibrate your thinking styles and unlock your innate problem-solving power.

We each have ninety cubic inches of brain-processing capacity; the biggest brain-to-body ratio of any species that has ever lived on this planet. At the same time, we've also developed five powerful senses, which input an unfathomable amount of information—far more than even our big brains can process. So sometimes, especially when faced with stressful situations, we need to rely on mental shortcuts. It makes our computing efforts simpler when we have a formula to apply. For instance, if a problem comes up and I'm automatically looking inward for whom to blame, that saves me a lot of thinking. Or, if I can automatically zoom right to the worst-case scenario, that funnels my thoughts and energy into just one (albeit unhelpful) pathway.

These shortcuts can be very efficient in computing information. It seems they would be helpful in that regard, saving us time and mental energy. And indeed they do.

But there's a catch.

The thinking behind these mental shortcuts is often awfully wrong. This creates *thinking traps.*

The real problem with thinking traps is that they mess up our problem-solving capability. They confuse the situation and get in the way of our seeing the world accurately. If you can't see a problem clearly, you can't solve it effectively—and that's even

> "The signal that you've fallen into a thinking trap is the feeling of 'I've been here before.' A familiar unsolvable problem is a dead giveaway that problematic thinking is running the show."
>
> —Andrew

more stressful. Plus, thinking traps exacerbate our emotions, so you end up feeling even more of whichever (or whichever combination) of the Big 7 Emotions has you in its grip. Like powerful surges of emotions, thinking traps make stressful events even more stressful than they need to be.

There are seven common traps. As you read through these, try to identify the one that you fall into most often—or the

The 7 Thinking Traps

- **Personalizing**: instinctively blaming yourself when things go wrong

- **Externalizing**: instinctively blaming other people or circumstances when things go wrong

- **Maximizing and Minimizing**: maximizing the bad and minimizing the good to let the negative take over and define a situation and your outlook

- **Mind Reading**: expecting others to know what you're thinking without having to tell them

- **Overgeneralizing**: taking one piece of information and making a general rule about the world, another person, or yourself without evidence to support your findings

- **Pessimism**: taking a real problem and following an unlikely path to the worst-case scenario, and then getting stressed about it

- **Emotional Reasoning**: letting your thinking be led by your emotions and using your emotions as evidence that something is real

one that, when you get sucked in by it, causes the most havoc in your life. That's the one we want to focus on first.

Let's take a look at each one in action and how it hinders our problem-solving powers.

You discover that your teenage son has taken out your car without asking. You go up to his room, knock on the door, and have a major blowup that leaves both of you upset. By all measures, a stressful situation. What's your takeaway?

A person who falls into the **Personalizing** trap would immediately blame him- or herself that the argument got so heated and think, "I've been on edge lately, and it's made me prickly with my family." Personalizing allows you to only see one source of the problem: what you believe you did to cause the situation. Blocked from your view are the causes attributable to circumstances or other people. If you're only seeing a subset of causes, you're only seeing a subset of solutions and missing out on the whole range of possible resolutions. Add to this the emotions that come with personalizing—guilt, shame, sadness, or embarrassment—which further cloud your thinking and you can see why this trap prevents you from solving problems effectively.

A person who falls into the **Externalizing** trap would do the exact opposite and point blame at their son for the blowup, perhaps jumping right to, "He's been disrespectful and prickly lately." The same dynamic is at work here as with personalizing, except this time, externalizers see only what the other person did or what the circumstances brought upon them, which means they are not seeing their role in the scenario. This puts the locus of control of the problem outside of themselves and removes their ability to effect change in the situation. All else being equal, it's easier to change something in you than it is to change something outside of yourself. To add to the tangle, as we know, that feeling "out of control" brings with it the emotional upheaval of frustration over not having the resources you need or the ability to make things go your way.

Maximizer/Minimizers might think, "My relationship with my kid is a disaster," while completely overlooking the great time they had with their son just that morning. Maximizer/minimizers often find themselves in an endless loop of problems that seem to show up wherever they go. For instance, they come away from their workweek thinking their job sucks. They resign, go to another job, and find that that one sucks, too, because they take their familiar habit of maximizing the bad/minimizing the good with them. They ditch one relationship because all they can see is the bad but not the good. But, of course, the next one will feel unsatisfying, as well, because they carry themselves wherever they go. They can't solve the "finding the right job or relationship" problem because it's really an internal thinking trap that's to blame.

> **WHEN IS A TRAP NOT A TRAP?:** A thinking trap is defined by the fact that there is no evidence to support your thinking. So, for instance, if you've been in the same relationship for twenty years and every day when you get home you ask your partner to give you a few minutes to chill out before they give you the to-do list, and yet every day when you walk in the door your partner hands you that list first thing, that's not a thinking trap. You are, indeed, not being given what you explicitly said you need.

If you fall into a **Mind Reading** trap, you might think something like, "I have a lot going on at work right now, and he should know I don't need this kind of conflict from him." Stuck in this trap, you throw your valuable energies into fighting phantoms. The other person likely doesn't know what you're thinking, and truth be told, you can't be sure what they are thinking. You can create an entire argument in your head without ever addressing the person. Needless to say, this is not an effective way to solve a relationship conflict, and usually adds to your stress by stirring up a maelstrom of imagined insults and offenses.

Overgeneralizing is often combined with personalizing or externalizing. For instance, in this case, "He never listens to me. He's impossible" or "I'm a lousy parent." Both thoughts put you in lockdown. They're much more difficult to do something about than, for instance, "I've been tired lately and not responding well" or "My kid needs to learn better manners." By definition, problems that are very general are more difficult to solve. One is something you can tackle, the other is an immovable state of being that leads to helplessness and hopelessness. Again, you're only seeing a subset of solutions, and in this case, it's the subset that is least likely to effect change.

A **Pessimism** trap creates a downward spiral that leads you to the worst-case scenario. It could generate thoughts like, "If he took the car without asking, what else is going on that I don't know about? What's wrong with him? He's going to end up getting into trouble at school or, worse, with the law. Then he won't get into a good college, and his future will be ruined."

Look, bad things do happen in life. We don't want to convert you from a pessimist to a Pollyanna; just from pessimism to realism. When you focus on the worst case, you allot the majority of your energy to worrying about something that has a one in a million chance of actually coming true. That's not a good deployment of resources. We want to spend our energy on the contingencies that are most likely to happen. If we get bogged down in stressing over the worst-case scenario, we miss the actual problems that come our way and end up, ironically, unprepared to deal with them. At the same time, there may be good possible outcomes at our disposal, but we're failing to see the positives and maximize them.

In the **Emotional Reasoning** trap, the thinking revolves around holding how you feel as absolute proof that what you perceive is unequivocally the reality. We have already seen from Day 1 that a lot of our feelings are unwarranted and based on mistaken beliefs. The thought causes the feeling. When we rely on those same feelings as proof that the thoughts are indeed real, we set ourselves up for an error in logic.

If you feel anxious, it's because you are thinking there is a future threat in evidence. But in fact, that may just be your anxiety radar pinging. Take meQuilibrium member Beth, forty-nine, for example. When her son strikes out on the ball field, she immediately worries he won't be chosen for the team. That feeling may or may not be warranted; however, just because Beth feels anxious when he strikes out doesn't guarantee that he won't get chosen. Believing that it does is emotional reasoning.

Emotional reasoning is a circular trap, because it keeps the emotion

"I was giving a presentation, and one of the attendees was staring out the window. I immediately thought, 'Oh no, I must not have prepared enough to make this engaging.' After, one of my colleagues said to me, 'I can't believe that jerk wasn't listening to you!' It really drove home for me how we all make our own weather. I immediately personalized while my colleague externalized. For all we know, the offender was stressed because he had a dentist appointment."

—Jan

in place. This applies to whatever emotion you're experiencing. In this particular circumstance, if you're angry, then that's your confirmation that your teenager violated your rights. If you feel guilty, you'll hold it as proof that you're to blame for the blowup between you. If you feel sad, it may trigger the belief that you're losing touch with your teenager or that your relationship just isn't as strong as you thought it was (the ideal/real gap).

Take Action

The good news is that for each thinking trap, there is a specific and actionable escape route to lead you back to serenity and sanity.

Choose the one that feels the most germane to you; it's a good place to start. While you may fall into all of the traps at one time or another, choosing the one (or at most two) that causes the greatest havoc in your life will yield you the biggest return without being too taxing. Remember, we take these mental shortcuts because our ninety cubic inches of brain space are overwhelmed, so it will only make things worse if you are scanning your thinking for all seven of these. Familiarize yourself with the escape route for your most common trap so that you're prepared the next time (today, perhaps?) you fall into it.

ESCAPE A PERSONALIZING TRAP

Personalizers experience sadness, guilt, shame, and embarrassment. When these emotions surface, ask yourself the following: *"I must be blaming myself for this problem, and though in part that might be true, what else is going on here? What's one thing that someone else did—or that circumstances created—that contributed to this problem, and what's one thing I can do about that?"* This helps bring some much-needed balance to the situation and broadens your perspective. Three-quarters of getting out of a thinking trap is escaping the tunnel vision it creates, blocking options from your view.

For example, meQuilibrium member Robin, thirty-eight, is a classic personalizer. If she texts a friend and doesn't get a response pronto, she starts to think that maybe her friend is upset with her. She becomes preoccupied, wondering if she has done something wrong or hurt her friend's feelings somehow. This leads her to feel sadness, shame, and guilt, which just further mucks up her day. But equipped with her newfound ability to escape the cloudy thinking caused by personalizing, Robin is able to come up with other possible causes, as well. Perhaps her friend is just busy right now. Maybe her friend just has a different response rate to text messages and doesn't have the quick trigger that Robin has. Maybe she isn't near her phone. This new thinking puts her in a calmer place until her friend finds the time to respond, saving her needless angst that only adds to her stress.

ESCAPE AN EXTERNALIZING TRAP

As with personalizing, externalizing is easier to detect through our emotions than our thoughts. The telltale emotions that signal you may have fallen into an externalizing trap are anger and frustration. The next time you feel angry and frustrated when confronted with a stressful situation, say the following to yourself: *"Okay, I am blaming other people or circumstances for this problem right now, and that could be true. But what's one thing that I did to contribute to this problem and one thing I can do about it right now?"*

Again, broader perspective means you are free to see the problem from all angles and have more resources to solve it. You put the locus of control back into your realm and from there can take effective action.

> **"BUT IT REALLY *IS* THEIR FAULT!"**: We want to assure all you externalizers out there that we really do understand. A teenager who takes an unsanctioned joyride in your car, the colleague who didn't get you the materials in time to complete your project, or the inconsiderate driver who cuts you off on the highway do, indeed, bear responsibility in the situation. But if that's where the story begins and ends for you, then you're stuck with the problem—and with the frustration and anger.
>
> Sometimes anger is warranted, and we don't necessarily need to let it go. But externalizing (and personalizing) is a lot like a broken watch: two times a day you might be right, but most of the time, you'll be wrong in your assessment—or, at the very least, incomplete in your understanding of the causes of the problem and, hence, of its numerous possible solutions.

ESCAPE A MAXIMIZING AND MINIMIZING TRAP

Remember, maximizing and minimizing color your outlook, so all you can see is the negative in a situation. Talk about a trap! For those of you who tend to maximize and minimize, we have a simple strategy. It may sound a little hokey as you read it, but we have proof that it works.

At the end of the day today, write down three good things that happened to you from the time you woke up until now. They don't have to be earth-shattering events; they can be as simple as discovering no line at Starbucks when you went to get your morning coffee or your kid scoring a goal in her soccer game. Tomorrow, right after you rub the sleep from your eyes, before you make breakfast, check e-mail, go to the gym, or do anything else, read those three things. That's all; just read them, and then go about your business.

At the end of tomorrow, do the same thing. Write down three more good things that happened to you that day, adding them to that same list. The next morning, read those six things. Do this exercise for ten days, and by the end, you'll have thirty good things written. You will very quickly find that by seeking out the good, you will have recalibrated your mind to become more attuned to the positive. We recommend doing this for ten days initially, and repeating it whenever you feel yourself being pulled back into habitual negative thinking.

ESCAPE A MIND READING TRAP

Gigi, thirty-one, was harboring a decent amount of resentment toward her husband regarding her not getting enough alone time amidst their busy family schedule. Eventually— and unsurprisingly—she lashed out one day and fumed, "This is ridiculous. All I want is to be able to go to yoga on Saturday mornings . . . is that too much to ask?!"

Gigi's husband looked at her incredulously. He literally had *no idea* what she was talking about. In fact, he actually expected her to be at yoga on Saturday mornings and figured she just chose to blow it off. He didn't want to seem like he was bugging her if she had fallen off the fitness wagon, so he stayed quiet. The heat of the argument quickly dissipated when they saw the needless morass of misunderstanding that their mind reading had created.

If you're upset with another person or frustrated by what feels like an impasse in the relationship, there's a good chance that you may have fallen into the mind reading trap. This is because, in your mind, someone hasn't given you what you want. The problem, of course, is that you haven't asked for it. At holiday time, if your mother-in-law comes over and it drives you nuts that no matter what you do she tells you a better way to do it, that can make you stressed. But if you can articulate in some way that you're not really asking for advice but that her assistance would be great, then you're letting the air out of that relationship stress point—likely for both of you. Not saying what we really want or need can create stress for both sides.

The next time you find yourself feeling frustrated or angry with someone, ask yourself: *"Have I communicated what I want or need to this person clearly and adequately?"* When in doubt, speak up.

ESCAPE AN OVERGENERALIZING TRAP

The interesting thing about overgeneralizing is that it increases the intensity of our feelings. If we personalize, we may feel sad; if we personalize and overgeneralize, we'll feel *very* sad. If we externalize, we may feel angry. If we externalize and overgeneralize, we'll feel big anger—otherwise known as rage. Overgeneralizing is the equivalent of emotional kerosene.

To catch yourself overgeneralizing, listen for words like *never* or *always*, or for character-indicting words like *lazy*, *stupid*, or *jerk* (or worse). The bigger your theory about yourself, another person, or the world, the more evidence you need to support it. Ask yourself: *"Am I really being objective and fair here, or is this my usual thinking trap at work? Is this person really always/never as*

I'm labeling them? Am I really a lousy parent, or a good parent just having a bad day?"

ESCAPE A PESSIMISM TRAP

Think of the entry (and exit) to a pessimism trap as a spiral staircase. It begins with a single event, which leads to a thought . . . and then another thought . . . and another. Things get progressively worse—and it doesn't just spiral in a specific domain. The negativity spiral gets broader and broader, like a cyclone. Pessimism has a way of bleeding from one area of your life into another, too. Things aren't going well at home, so you're not sleeping well, which makes you worry that you won't perform well at work. And so on.

Take meQuilibrium member Jillian, fifty-eight, for example. Jillian owns a successful consulting firm, is highly regarded in her industry, and has amassed more than a comfortable nest egg. Yet when even the smallest thing goes wrong, she's convinced it'll all go down the tubes and she'll end up on the street.

Jillian explained her favorite and familiar spiral: "If I don't make a train to get into the city for a client meeting, I think I'm going to ultimately turn into a bag lady. I didn't book a seat on the train from Boston to New York to make it to the meeting . . . that means I won't land the project . . . and that means my reputation will be damaged, and my existing clients will leave . . . that means I won't be able to make payroll or pay for my mortgage or my children's college tuition . . . my business will fold, my family will crumble, and I'll go down the road to ruin." Each thought sets off another in a domino effect that knocks her down, even though she rationally knows none of it is logical. But we're human, with powerful human emotions that often override logic and reason.

With each thought, Jillian is counting on the worst-case scenario coming true. What she ultimately learned to do—and what you're about to learn, too—is to analyze the probability of the whole chain of events happening, instead of analyzing the probability of each event based on the event before. What's the probability that your perceived end result will occur based on that one triggering event? Okay, so she missed the train. Yes, that might mean that she could lose that particular client, but does that really also mean her reputation will go up in smoke and that she'll lose everything she's worked for and everyone she loves as a result?

By this point, the first time she did the exercise, Jillian was smiling, because she could see the absurdity of her thinking. When you get to the point that you can laugh at yourself a little, you've broken the spell. Then you can pull back and see what really happened, and you're calm and clearheaded enough to think of other solutions. In this particular case, there were many options at her disposal: she could think fast and book a seat on the shuttle flight, call the client and move the meeting by an hour, Skype into the meeting . . . anything but panic and go down the mental road to bag-lady-dom.

Think about a pessimism spiral you've had. How far down the rabbit hole did you go? What did you convince yourself would happen based on one triggering event?

EMOTIONAL REASONING

You've already seen that you can arrive at emotions through mistaken thinking. For instance, you may have gotten angry in a given situation, but if you then use your angry state as proof that your rights have been violated, that's emotional reasoning.

You're anxious, so you're convinced that means something bad is going to happen. But nope, it doesn't. It just means that you're anxious because there could be a negative outcome ahead, and the stakes feel high. It doesn't mean that the bad outcome necessarily will happen or, if it does, that it will be the worst possible outcome. You feel guilty, so you must have shafted someone else, right? Wrong. You just feel guilty.

The ladder up and out of an emotional reasoning trap is your new skill of Trap It, Map It, Zap It. Identify the emotion, find the thought-feed thought behind it, and ask yourself if the thought is real or if it's an imaginary ping picked up by your radar. When you burst the bubble of the emotion, you'll restore clarity and calm and be able to solve whatever problem is at hand.

ESCAPE A THINKING TRAP

THINKING TRAP	ESCAPE PLAN
Personalizing	Ask yourself, "What's one thing that someone else did—or that circumstances created—that contributed to this problem, and what's one thing I can do about that?"
Externalizing	Ask yourself, "What's one thing that I did to contribute to this problem and one thing I can do about it right now?"
Maximizing and Minimizing	List three good things that happened to you today, and review the growing list each morning for ten days.
Mind Reading	Ask yourself, "Have I communicated what I want or need to this person clearly and adequately?"
Overgeneralizing	Ask yourself, "Do I really have evidence to support such a general theory?"
Pessimism	Identify the triggering event; then ask yourself, "What's the probability that the end result will occur based on this one triggering event?"
Emotional Reasoning	Identify the emotion, and use Trap It, Map It, Zap It to determine if it is real and warranted or just a phantom generated by your emotion radar.

Your Future Action Plan

The more you can arm yourself in advance, the better. It's very useful to identify not only which thinking trap you fall into most but also the situations in which you are most vulnerable to it. Is it when something goes wrong at work, during a conflict with your spouse, when you encounter scheduling snafus? Think ahead and come up with one thing you can do to avoid falling into that thinking trap the next time that situation arises so that you can safeguard your problem-solving power.

My Plan for Escaping Thinking Traps

I choose to work on this skill because:

The thinking trap I most commonly fall into is:

The telltale signs that I have fallen into this trap are:

What I will do/say to myself to escape this trap:

The situation(s) in which I am most vulnerable to falling into this thinking trap are:

The one thing I can do to avoid falling into that trap in the future is:

Day Four

Access Instant Calm

Q *The Payoff: Immediate relief from high stress in pressure-cooker situations*

The big moment you've been preparing for is here. You're standing by the side of the stage, about to climb up to the podium and give a speech in front of one hundred people. No, make that one thousand people. You look out into the audience and see your mother-in-law, your boss, and, oh, let's throw in your high school gym teacher—all looking at you, expecting brilliance. You feel the anxiety rise as your face and arms go numb, your throat begins to constrict, and the pounding heartbeat in your ears grows louder and louder.

Is this a good time to pause and work on your emotion radar or thinking-trap skills? Heck, no!

Sure, you can use these tools to analyze the experience afterward, but right then and there, you need a quick relief. We've taught you a few skills already to tackle your thinking and rewire your stress response. But what about those moments of intense stress, when you just need to calm down *fast*? What do you do when you need to get that hammering heart rate and those shaking hands under control ASAP so that you can perform at your best?

Long-term change is what we're after, of course, but some-times you need an immediate tool to get yourself back on solid ground. While you're rewiring the thinking habits that generate overwhelming emotions, why not also pick up a few skills to tackle the emotions directly? This is a bandage, yes, but sometimes you need to just stop the bleeding and tend to healing the wound later.

Acute stress activates our sympathetic nervous system. It ramps up our bodies and brains to prepare us to fight or flee. Our hearts start to pound, muscles get tense, and throats get dry. Happily, our bodies also have a built-in relaxation re-sponse to counter this high-alert state: the parasympathetic nervous system. If we invoke the parasympathetic response, the fight-or-flight mechanism automatically shuts down. They are opponent physiologic processes; you cannot have both run-ning at the same time. The relaxation response is the ticket to instantaneous calm.

The relaxation response causes the release of soothing, plea-surable chemicals known as endorphins, which act as a potent antidote to adrenaline. This creates a physical state of deep rest that slows the heart rate and breathing, reduces blood pressure

CALM DOWN TO SLIM DOWN: In case you need another reason to learn how to access instant calm and dial down the stress: stress makes you fat. When the sympathetic nervous system is triggered, it floods your body with cortisol, otherwise known as the stress hormone. Part of cortisol's job is to stimulate the body to store fat, especially in the abdomen, to use as a quick energy source for the body. But because the "threats" we're responding to nowadays don't generally necessitate that we run for our lives, we're not using up these energy stores, so we're saving it up and packing on the pounds. To add insult to injury, belly fat is more than just a wardrobe bummer; it's linked to cardiovascular disease, type 2 diabetes, and stroke.

and stress hormones, and relaxes muscles. In addition to its calming physical effects, research shows that the relaxation response increases energy and focus, combats illness, relieves aches and pains, heightens problem-solving abilities, and boosts motivation, productivity, and feelings of happiness and peace.

Below are three skills you can learn to activate your parasympathetic nervous system to trigger relief in pressure-cooker situations.

Take Action

Read through each of these three skills to familiarize yourself with the steps. Then, the next time you find yourself in a highly charged situation, put them into practice and watch the stress bubble burst as quickly as it appeared.

Instant Calm Skill #1: Deep Breathing

Many people unconsciously go through the day taking short, shallow breaths. When we take in less oxygen, the heart has to pump faster to get the same amount of oxygenated blood to the vital organs—and an accelerated heart rate signals our brains that "anxiety" is afoot. When you take deep breaths from the abdomen, rather than shallow breaths from your upper chest, you inhale more oxygen and feel more relaxed.

Abdominal breathing will trigger your parasympathetic nervous system and enable you to regain equilibrium. The great thing about it is that you can do it anywhere that you need to access instant calm: at your desk, before a medical exam, when someone says something that upsets you.

Follow these simple steps:

1. Before you start, give yourself a trigger signal to tell your body you're about to practice. For example, touch your

breastbone or navel with your right hand, and tell your-self: "I am triggering my relaxation response." Repeat-ing your trigger signal each time conditions your nervous system to know what to expect and, over time, also cues your body to go into relaxation mode.

2. With your eyes open or closed, place your hand on your belly (if you are in a public place and would prefer to skip this step, that's perfectly okay).

3. Begin to control your breathing by taking a few deep, slow, comfortable breaths.

4. Take a deep breath in for four slow counts. Then breathe out, also slowly, for a count of four. Lung capacities vary, so four may not be your optimal number. You should feel your stomach rising about an inch as you breathe in and falling an inch when you breathe out. Find what works for you and practice until it feels like second nature.

With this breathing practice, you don't have to force any-thing; your body knows how to relax. Just take your deep breaths, and trust it to relax naturally. Don't worry if you're doing it right or wrong, and know that each session of relax-ation may feel different from the last one.

Instant Calm Skill #2: Progressive Muscle Relaxation
Again, our muscles tense when our sympathetic nervous sys-tem is activated to get our bodies ready to fight or flee. By relaxing those same muscles, we're sending the signal to the body that the threat is gone, which promotes the relaxation response.

Follow these steps:

1. Sit in a comfortable but sturdy chair. An office chair is fine, as long as it doesn't recline so far that you can lose your balance.

2. Breathe. Start by controlling your breathing (in for four counts, out for four counts).

3. Ball your hands into fists, and tighten and curl your toes and feet. Keep them tensed for a full eight-second breath count (four counts in, four counts out). Then release both and let them flop and relax, as if there were no bones in them at all, again for a full breath count of eight. Repeat until you can feel a faint, calming throb in your hands and feet (some people describe it as a humming or buzzing).

4. As you continue your controlled breathing, keeping your toes planted on the floor, lift your heels and tighten your calf muscles. Tense your forearms without tensing your hands—keep your hands open, palms down. Keep arms and calves tensed for a full breathing count of eight, and then let them flop for a count of eight. Repeat until they begin to gently throb.

5. As you continue your slow breathing, squeeze your thighs together and flex your biceps for a breathing count of eight, then let them flop for a full count of eight. Repeat until they begin to gently throb.

6. Repeat this process with abs, then chest, and then finally your neck. The key is to do it in the same sequence every time. The body learns what to expect and will already begin to relax the later muscles while you work on the first.

With practice, you'll instinctively know how long your deep, controlled breath lasts and won't need to keep count anymore. The whole process should only take a few minutes. Eventually, you'll also be able to work through the progression faster, which gets you back on track faster, too. But remember: Speed is not the goal. Feeling relaxed and reenergized is.

Instant Calm Skill #3: Positive Imagery

Picture yourself sitting on a warm beach at your favorite vacation spot. The sun is shining; the sky is sparkling blue. A gentle breeze wafts over you, carrying the scent of ocean air and coconut lotion. You take a sip of a delicious, cold drink as you crack open the new book you've been looking forward to reading. Your family is off doing something they enjoy; everyone healthy and safe. Stretching before you is a leisurely two hours in which you have nowhere to be and no one looking for you.

How do you feel?

Positive imagery is a particularly powerful and transformative tool, because it involves all your senses. You can instantaneously cut off the sympathetic nervous system by shifting your mind from threat to treat. That doesn't mean, of course, that escapism is a long-term fix. If you're facing a crisis in your job and spend the entire day dreaming about a vacation on the beach, that isn't going to solve the problem. But pausing to invoke a positive image in your mind will unhook you from the adrenaline spike and allow you to ratchet down the stress. Then you can calmly face the challenge at hand.

Follow these steps:

1. Begin by conjuring up a place and time when you felt completely at peace. A real memory works best because you can imagine it more vividly.

2. Recall the scene, employing as many of your five senses as you can, as if you are still there. Write down what you remember, in detail, keeping the story in the present tense as though you are still in the scene. You can use these questions as a guide to trigger your sense memory, conjuring up what you see, feel, smell, taste, and hear:

▷ Where were you? (on a mountaintop, celebrating with my whole family at my parents' fiftieth wedding anniversary)

▷ What were you doing? (sitting in a deck chair, hiking, dancing)

▷ What do you smell? (freshly cut grass, cookies baking in the oven)

▷ What do you hear? (crashing waves, a sizzling grill, music, my children laughing)

▷ What can you feel/touch? (sun on my face, warm sand between my toes)

▷ What can you taste? (tangy barbecue, hot cocoa with marshmallows, sweet ripe strawberries)

▷ What can you see? (palm trees, blue ocean, twinkling stars in an inky-blue sky)

Here is a wonderful example from meQuilibrium member Martin, sixty-three:

"I'm on my favorite golf course with my favorite golfing buddy. It's just about sunset and we're walking toward the eighteenth tee. I've had a great game—looks like I'll break eighty. The sun is behind the trees, and there's a red glow across the sky. The evening breeze has just picked up, and I can feel it on my skin. It feels really good since I got a lot of sun earlier in the day. I can smell the fresh-cut grass. The thicker grass of the fairway springs under my golf shoes. As I strike the ball, I can feel the smack through my hands and my forearms. I can almost taste that refreshing beer we'll have in the clubhouse together when we've finished the round."

Pay attention to how you feel as you recall and record this sense memory. Do you feel the stress ebbing away? This sense of tranquility is available to you any time you need it. The next time you're overwhelmed by stress, close your eyes and take this mental breather to quickly reset your equilibrium. You don't necessarily need to write it down the next time, unless doing so helps you even more than conjuring it up in your mind. What ultimately matters is that you pause and imagine the scene fully using all five senses. Within moments, you'll feel calm wash over you.

Cultivate Long-Term Calm

You many not have realized it, but the three skills you are learning here today are some of the building blocks of meditation—one of the proven methods for long-term stress management. Studies show that meditating for even a few minutes a day can have a huge positive impact on your health, well-being, and stress level. It can reduce high blood pressure, anxiety, binge eating, fatigue, pain, sleep problems, heart disease, and substance abuse.

Even better, the practice of meditation produces a tranquil mind and cultivates introspection. It will help you notice—and block—serious stress before it takes hold. You can learn more about how to begin an easy meditation practice at www.mequilibrium.com.

My Plan to Access Instant Calm

I choose to work on the skill of accessing instant calm because:

The skill I will use the next time I am in a high-pressure situation is:

The positive imagery I will use, when I deploy that skill, is:

Day Five

Refuel the Right Way

 The Payoff: Improved stamina, better health, and immunity against toxic stress

On a purely biological level, the old adage "You are what you eat" is as true today as ever. It's pretty straightforward: if you fuel your brain cells, vital organs, and muscles with nutritious, vibrant foods, they're better equipped to rally in your defense. Inundate them with processed junk, trans fats, and sugar and you're making it abundantly harder on yourself to manage stressful situations. It's pretty tough to think clearly and have the energy to rise to challenges when you're feeling sluggish. And forget having the spark to grab hold of exciting opportunities that come your way and dial your life into the positive!

Today we're going to arm you with powerful (but surprisingly easy to use) tools to get control of your eating habits, improve your stamina, and give you the energy and focus to combat the challenges that come your way.

> "Diet and nutrition can either be your best allies or your worst enemies when it comes to fighting stress."
>
> —Adam

Feeding Stress

Eating an excess of unhealthy food does more than pack on unwanted pounds. When we eat poorly, we trigger harmful inflammation in our bodies for up to three hours after eating (inflammation has been connected to a myriad of ailments, including heart disease, Alzheimer's, and cancer). Once in a while, that's okay, but do it repeatedly and that's when your body breaks down. Life is about balance.

Let's say you start your morning with a breakfast of bacon, egg, and cheese on a buttery croissant. Before you even get into the groove of your day, you've triggered the inflammatory process. Your system will start to calm down from the breakfast-sparked inflammation roughly around lunchtime, but then let's imagine you go and do it all over again with fast food and soda. That's adding an interior stress bomb on top of whatever stress you have from workday hassles. Things might calm down in your body once again a few hours later—or you retrigger it once more at the end of the day with a large pepperoni pizza with extra cheese for dinner. Cap it off with your middle schooler's meltdown over algebra homework that night, and suddenly, you find yourself in a chronic state of inflammation and stress.

That's the bad news. But here's the good: our research has shown that making just a few changes and gaining control here has a strong spillover effect in every other area of your life.

A clergy association in North Carolina came to us not long ago for help. Their members were not doing well physically or psychologically, showing signs of extreme stress. They were overweight, overworked, and burned out, experiencing all the problems that come with poor food choices and lack of exercise. We put thirty-five of these members through the meQuilibrium program, and within thirty days they showed improvement on three important variables: they were no longer eating more when stressed, they were making healthier food decisions, and they were exercising better and smarter. That in and of itself was a win, but the benefits didn't end there. They also showed a corresponding boost in their ability to regulate their emotions and change the thinking habits that were clouding their judgment and ability to focus on work. In fact, it was these changes in resilience that powered their better physical health habits; the clergy members' ability to dispel negative thoughts and keep emotions regulated was the key to their being able to maintain better physical health. Again, you can see how it's all interconnected.

There's another big factor to consider in the link between what we eat and stress management: self-esteem. The choices we make are what have the greatest impact on how we feel about ourselves. When we have the resolve to make good food choices, we feel strong, virtuous, and in control. We possess confidence in our ability to determine our own destiny.

Conversely, when we consistently make unhealthy food choices (or go unconscious entirely, wondering how it came to pass that we ate that third helping of macaroni and cheese), we can feel guilty, ashamed, sad, or embarrassed. How many times have you berated yourself for eating a donut in the break room just because it was there? Or been disappointed in yourself for overindulging at a holiday party? These particular negative emotions, when activated chronically, can cause a big hit to our self-esteem.

We could load you up with all kinds of scientific explanations for why powering your body with the right foods helps combat stress, and why eating the wrong ones does the exact opposite, but the proof, really, is in the experience. You've been living in your body long enough to know how you feel when you eat poorly and how you feel when you choose healthy, energizing foods.

We're not here to tell you not to enjoy your mother's famous lasagna or your favorite decadent dessert. Treats like these are among life's greatest pleasures! Instead, we want to help you become mindful of the food choices you make *on an everyday basis* so that when you do indulge, you do it consciously and joyfully. We want to put you back in control so that you can regain balance and peace of mind.

Take Action

There are two things you'll accomplish today: learn to *eat mindfully* and learn to *eat better.* When done in tandem, these two habits will turn your body into a powerful ally against stress.

EAT MINDFULLY

If you've tried to get control of your eating habits before, without success, you might be skeptical that we can tell you anything new. But there's a reason that up until now your goals and behaviors haven't lined up. If you're not mindful of the decisions you're making—not just about what you're eating but about *why*—it's hard to really accomplish any health-related goals.

Most people mean to eat well. But what happens to your good intentions when you're under stress, have other things on your mind, or even when you're bored? Like many people, your resolutions for healthy eating probably vanish as quickly as that warm slice of apple pie à la mode. You eat unhealthy food—or even just overeat good food—without giving it a second thought. Then you're left feeling bloated, guilty, and more stressed than before.

This is called *unconscious eating*. Humans are creatures of habit. By definition, habits are unconscious: we do them without thinking. This can be a double-edged sword. If the habit is good—that is, if the behavior is good for us and gets us closer to our goals, like putting a big bottle of water on your desk to sip from throughout the day—it saves us mental energy that we can apply to everything else we have going on.

On the flip side, a bad habit can take us away from our goals, like when you munch your way through a large bag of chips while watching television at night. When a habit is unconscious, it doesn't appear on your radar for closer scrutiny. We need to become conscious of habits before we can change them.

To go from mindless to mindful eating, you first need to discover what kind of unconscious eater you are. There are two kinds of unconscious eating: emotional eating and multitask eating. Which of these rings most true for you?

Emotional Eating: I rely on food to lift my mood when I'm feeling sad, anxious, frustrated, angry, guilty, stressed, or bored.

Multitask Eating: I eat meals or snacks while in front of the television, reading, driving, talking on the phone, or in bed.

If the answer isn't immediately apparent, you can track your eating habits over the past few days. Take note: Did you binge? Did you eat too much or eat when you weren't really hungry? What were you doing or feeling when that happened?

Why We Overeat

Deep in our human past, our ancestors needed to go out and hunt for food. It was a difficult, perilous task that involved bringing down large prey, risking attack from other tribes, and dealing with rough terrain and unkind weather. These early humans needed a drive strong enough to force them out of their safe, warm caves. Enter *hunger*.

But even food-seekers driven by hunger weren't always successful, and they couldn't count on three squares a day. The meat, wild fruits, and vegetables they did find couldn't easily be stored for later, so they learned to consume everything, right then and there. You see where this is going, don't you? We are heirs to the instincts of those hungry early plate-cleaners.

The problem is that, today, food is constantly available, and our relatively sedentary lifestyle requires us to eat less of it to store for fuel. Unfortunately, our instincts haven't evolved with our lifestyles, so we overeat.

The good news: Our brains can change. Our caveman programming, though deep, is no match for our powerful minds if and when we consciously choose to change. With the right psychological tools, like the ones you are learning today, you can rewire your caveman brain and gain control.

Once you identify which kind of emotional eater you are, you can learn techniques to avoid falling into the same old trap.

Emotional Eating
Eating feels good. It activates the pleasure centers in your brain, so it can distract you when you're feeling anxious or

worried. When you find yourself swimming in a stormy sea of negative emotions, a glazed donut can act like a life preserver to keep you afloat.

But food is a quick fix without lasting benefits. Once the "food high" of a binge wears off, you're left with the same stressor . . . plus some guilt, harmful inflammation, and, often, digestive discomfort. Unfortunately, this fix can become an addiction with serious consequences, so we need to fix the emotional reason you turn to food to break the cycle.

Follow these steps to free yourself from the habit of emotional eating:

1. Trap the Emotion. If you're an emotional eater, the bingeing is a symptom of a negative emotion. The next time you find yourself looking for a food fix, hit PAUSE. It's an opportunity to use your emotion-radar skill to get to the feeling behind the impulse. Tune in to your physical sensations: Do you feel the heavy weight of sadness? The flutter of anxiety? (If the binge has already happened, it's still an opportunity; look back and track how you were feeling right before to find the trigger.)

2. Map the Emotion. Map the emotion to the circumstance in which it showed up. Was it when you were angry about something your spouse said? Anxious in a social setting? Bored? Try to identify the specific thought feed behind the emotion.

3. Zap the Thought. Challenge those thoughts that fuel your emotional eating. Here are some common emotional eating thoughts and some ideas on how to challenge them:

Thought: "I need this food to feel better."

Thought Zapper: "That's not true. Food only gives me a fake, short high. When that wears off, I'll be back to feeling the same negative emotion."

Thought: "I do feel better after I eat it, so it must be working."

Thought Zapper: "That's not true. Eating simply activates the pleasure centers in my brain, so it temporarily blunts negative emotions. Even worse, overeating makes me feel ashamed."

Thought: "If I don't eat this, I'll feel worse."

Thought Zapper: "That's not true. Feeling the emotion will enable me to better tackle it directly."

Thought: "But I'm hungry . . ."

Thought Zapper: "Do I feel true hunger on a physiological level? Or am I just angry/anxious/sad/looking for something to do?"

Multitask Eating

Eating while you're doing something else is so easy to do. Breakfast in the car on the way to work, browsing online while eating lunch . . . you might think these are time-savers. The problem is that you're compromising another precious resource in the process: your physical well-being.

We can't perform another task and monitor how much we eat at the same time, so we consume more than we're aware of, at a faster rate. This scrambles the hunger/satiety signals in your body. There are several methods by which the body signals satiety, like a distended stomach and the release of the hormone leptin (the body's natural appetite control). If we're eating quickly, by the time our body picks up on these signals, we've already eaten too much.

You remember Pavlov's dogs? In this famous experiment, dogs were given food just after they heard the jingling of keys to open their cages, and eventually, they began salivating as soon as they heard the jingle, whether they got food or not.

Similarly, if you frequently snack while watching television, you'll start looking for food as soon as you tune in, whether you're hungry or not. Psychologists call this *classical conditioning*. It's the reason why we automatically crave popcorn or licorice the instant we enter a movie theater.

A Happy End to Emotional Eating

Jan is probably one of our best examples of how the skills you're learning here can help you escape from entrenched emotional eating:

> I can tell you the details of every popular diet trend of the last fifteen years, but knowing that stuff wasn't nearly as helpful as understanding why it is that if I'm in an airport coming home from a business trip and my flight home is delayed, I have to buy a bag of pretzels. It has nothing to do with hunger. I'm feeling lonely or worried that I'm letting down the people at home, so I need some comfort. Knowing that has allowed me to say, "Okay, I understand I'm lonely, but I'll have a cup of tea instead. Or better yet, I'll call them." Keeping these skills in the front of my mind has really accelerated lifestyle changes in a radically different way than before. I'm in better shape, I can manage my emotions . . . and there are no more pretzels in airports.

The good news is that, unlike Pavlov's dogs, you can teach yourself skills to counteract your conditioning. Follow these steps to break the cycle of multitask eating:

1. Trap the Habit. Where and when do you multitask eat? Is it eating cookies while reading in bed, dinner in front of the TV, lunch in your cubicle while you work? Think back over the last few days, and list the times and places in which you ate while you were doing something else.

2. Map the Habit. Look over your list from the previous step, and place a total ban on the places you multitask eat: on the couch, in the car, in bed. As of today, declare no more food allowed in those spots. Identify the activities and ban eating during those, too: watching TV, driving, and so on. If you're in any of those places or doing any of those activities, simply postpone eating. That takes us to the second part of this step. Create designated eating areas, such as the kitchen table, the cafeteria at work, or even a park bench, where you will eat and—this is key—*not do anything else at the same time*. Just enjoy your meal or snack without distraction. This breaks the place/activity/food association.

3. Zap the Habit. Challenge the thoughts that come up when you are tempted to multitask eat. Here are some common ones and some ideas on how to challenge them:

Thought: "I can't enjoy TV/reading/the movies without a snack. Not snacking will suck all the enjoyment and fun out of it."

Thought Zapper: "That's not true. Those activities are fun by themselves. It's just that I've come to associate them with food. If other people can have fun doing those things without eating at the same time, then I can, too."

Thought: "Eating while doing something else saves me time."
Thought Zapper: "How much time am I saving, really? Is it worth it to sabotage my health and weight just to shave off a few minutes?"

Thought: "I can keep track of how much I eat, even if I'm doing something else."
Thought Zapper: "It's not possible to give full focus to two things at one time, so even if I think I'm paying attention, I'm probably not accurate in my assessment."

> **BE YOUR CHANGE:** One of Jan's guiding principles is that your perception creates your reality. This belief is especially useful for changing our physical habits.
>
> For instance, when Jan decided she wanted to stop eating chips (and she loves chips) and choose a healthier snack, she didn't say, "I must never eat a chip again." Instead she went with positive imagery: "I am a goddess, and goddesses don't eat chips." If you know what you are and what you do as a result, then you know what you won't do. You can make the change by being what you want to become—which is far easier than wrestling with empty willpower. Chips are no match for a goddess armed with mental conviction!

EAT BETTER

Okay, so now that you know *how* to eat (mindfully), let's talk about *what* to eat!

There are a lot of good nutrition plans out there. Diets come and go in terms of popularity, and depending on your genetic predisposition, personal taste, and daily schedule, one or another may be best for you. Ultimately, it's for you to experiment and decide what feels best.

Having said that, what we know about food and nutrition today is revolutionary compared to where we were as a culture as recently as twenty years ago. Breakthrough nutritional science has revealed simple, comprehensive guidelines for making smart food choices, which Dr. Adam reveals below. Knowing these guidelines changes the process from "What do I feel like having?" to "What would make me feel good, strong, and healthy?" When we approach our menu that way, we have the win-win of tastes good *and* does us good.

Dr. Adam's Prescription for Eating Smart

- Keep an eye on the calorie count and quality. While you don't need to track everything that goes into your mouth, you want to have a general idea of how much you're eating and make sure that the calories you're taking in are nutritious.

- Omit the "whites." Carbohydrates help your brain produce the calming and mood-boosting neurotransmitter serotonin, but not all carbs are created equal. Complex carbs, such as those found in whole grains, are a better choice than simple or refined carbs (white sugar, white flour, and the like), because they are good sources of vitamins, fiber, and minerals.

- Avoid fried foods. These are loaded with unhealthy fats that contribute to heart disease.

- Skip the soda. Soda is wasted calories (sparkling water and seltzer are okay). And studies have proven a correlation between soda intake and type 2 diabetes.

- Pack your plate with color. Aim for a colorful assortment of fruits and vegetables in your daily diet. The more variety, the better.

- Go lean on the protein. Cut back on red meat, and include more cold-water fish in your diet, like salmon.

- Slash the salt. Use spices instead; it's an easy swap.

- Avoid partially hydrogenated oils. Read labels and steer clear of these unhealthy fats.

- Make it easy on yourself. Clear your shelves of the junk food that you tend to crave, and replace it with healthier alternatives, such as whole-grain snacks, fruit, and yogurt.

- Create portions. Divvy out your meal or snack ahead of time. Sitting down with an open bag of chips or a box of chocolates only tempts you to keep on eating.

- Read labels. It's important to know what's in the food you're eating. Keep an eye out for high sugar content, hydrogenated fats, high fructose corn syrup, and excess calories.

- Take a pause. When you've eaten half the portion, stop eating for a few minutes. Breathe. Reflect. Have a conversation with your dining companions. Allow your body time to signal to your brain that you're full. If, after you pause, you are not full, then go ahead and eat the second half, but no more. If you are feeling full, then wrap the plate for later. When you make a good eating decision, be sure to revel in the sense of pride that comes along with it.

Stress-Busting Foods

Additionally, include plenty of foods that are helpful for fighting stress. Choose ones that contain these powerful vitamins and minerals to bolster your body and mind (think "BMOC" to help you remember):

- B Vitamins. This class of vitamins, which includes B6, B12, and folate—is essential to the production of anxiety-easing and pleasure-inducing neurotransmitters, such as serotonin, GABA, and dopamine. Foods rich in B vitamins include chickpeas, lentils, yellowfin tuna, green beans, milk, plain yogurt, salmon, chicken, asparagus, and oatmeal.

- Magnesium. Magnesium, like B vitamins, also helps produce the calming neurotransmitters GABA and dopamine. But it's also a good muscle relaxant. Foods loaded with magnesium include almonds, amaranth, spinach, sunflower seeds, tofu, and wild rice.

- Omega-3s. A deficiency in these crucial fatty acids has been linked to depression and mood swings. They're also the go-to foods to reduce inflammation, which, as you now know, can be triggered by stress. Since your body doesn't produce omega-3s, it's important to make them part of your regular diet. Good sources of omega-3s are salmon, sardines, oysters, halibut, flax, and walnuts.

- Vitamin C. When you're feeling stressed, your body produces the hormone cortisol, which causes you to put on harmful belly fat. Worse, too much cortisol over the long term can lead to brain cell damage. Vitamin C may help prevent this kind of cellular damage, while at the same time keeping your immune system strong. To up your intake of vitamin C, include broccoli, Brussels sprouts, orange juice, red and green peppers, and strawberries in your diet.

With today's skill under your belt, you're well on your way to improving your eating habits and taking control of your physical health. Take a moment to really let that sink in. No more frustration, no more trying to eat right and failing or giving up. You're now armed with the tools that will enable you to become conscious of your habits and break the ones that aren't serving you. Where before refueling the right way may have been a struggle, you're now starting to understand that, when it comes to making changes, you're running the show.

My Plan for Refueling the Right Way

I choose to work on this skill because:

The type of unconscious eater I am is:

My plan for overcoming that style of unconscious eating is:

The healthy changes from Dr. Adam's list I will try are:

I will include more of these stress-busting foods in my diet:

Day Six

Navigate Around Iceberg Beliefs

 The Payoff: Control over emotional outbursts and a deeper seat of calm

Have you ever experienced a really big emotional outburst, from which you walked away wondering, "Where did *that* come from?" If you answered yes, you're in good company. Almost everyone has at one time or another. Here are a few choice ones from meQuilibrium members:

> *"I kicked a parking meter and yelled at the traffic cop who gave me a ticket for being two minutes past expiration."*
>
> —Robert, fifty-three

> *"When the tech guy at the computer store told me it would take a week to fix my laptop, I burst into tears in the middle of the store—like, the loud, gulping kind of crying."*
>
> —Nalani, twenty-seven

> *"I got a phone call from my son at school, asking me to pick him up because he wasn't feeling well, but I had to be in an important meeting in fifteen minutes. I went into a wild panic trying to figure out what to do."*
>
> —Eve, forty-two

These supercharged eruptions happen when we unknowingly crash into *iceberg beliefs*: big beliefs we have about ourselves, our world, and our future. Today you're going to discover how to unearth your icebergs and reroute your thinking when you hit one to quiet the emotional storm.

The Evolution of Icebergs

We've talked a lot up until now about the impact of faulty thinking on our emotions. But what about the power of our beliefs? You know, those bone-deep assumptions we have about how things should be. What happens if they're not accurate?

The two founding fathers of cognitive therapy, Albert Ellis and Aaron "Tim" Beck, both noted that faulty assumptions can get in the way of our happiness, productivity, and overall experience of success in life. Ellis called these "irrational beliefs," and Beck referred to them as "underlying assumptions."

In his work at the University of Pennsylvania, Andrew began to see that these beliefs acted much like icebergs, in that 99 percent of them lay hidden, and he and his colleagues named them as such. The tip of the iceberg was our conscious awareness, but the rest—our subconscious mind—was what was usually running the show. Andrew and his colleagues developed a step-by-step system to help people get to the icebergs below the surface and, even more important, learn to navigate around them. That's what you're going to learn today.

If an emotional surge is so powerful that it takes you by surprise, you're likely bumping up against an iceberg belief. Andrew explains that icebergs usually show up as rules about how we believe things should be and how we, and others, should behave. For instance, "The world should be fair" or "I need to be a perfect parent." Sometimes they are conditional, as in, "If I can't do something my way, I won't do it at all."

We begin to develop these rules from the time we're cognizant, which is basically birth. By the time we're ten years old, they're very strongly formulated. As adults, we don't even know we're still carrying them around; that's how ingrained they are and how hidden beneath the surface of our daily lives. If

ICEBERG BELIEFS: Big beliefs we have about ourselves, our world, and our future; they usually show up as rules about how we believe things should be and how we, and others, should behave.

we did stumble upon them somehow, we might laugh at how outdated they sound, but it's as though that memo didn't make the rounds to every department in our grown-up brains.

Let's say, as the oldest of six siblings, you developed the belief that "I need to always be in charge or things will go wrong." It sounds silly when you say it out loud, as though it can't possibly be true. But if you didn't believe it, you wouldn't be running yourself ragged trying to control everything. The proof is in our behavior, which, remember, is *always* fueled by our thoughts.

Cracking the code on your icebergs can be a serious game changer in your life. They may very well be creating your schedule chaos, getting in your way of successfully sticking to a diet, or holding you back from seizing opportunities. If you have an iceberg that dictates that you should be all things to all people, there's no doubt you're doing way more than even the mightiest of superheroes could take on (and, as a result, heaping a world of stress onto your shoulders). If you believe your family comes first in all circumstances, it's unlikely you'll willingly take time away from tending to their needs to care for yourself (which affects your health and overall resilience). If you have an iceberg that says you should avoid embarrassment at all costs, chances are you will shy away from trying new things (keeping you stuck in neutral, at best).

Iceberg beliefs are deeply rooted and powerful, and they fuel our emotions. The more entrenched an iceberg is, the more havoc it wreaks on your life—and, conversely, the more benefit you get by melting it. If we get a handle on our icebergs, we gain an *enormous* amount of control over our feelings and our lives. Melt an iceberg and all the downstream events it causes get washed away, as well.

Take, for instance, Meagan, age forty-two. Meagan noticed that anxiety was creeping in for her during a number of situations, and she struggled to understand why. She's not normally an anxious person and doesn't worry about a lot of things, but over the years, she noticed that her voice would quiver if she had to speak out loud at PTA meetings, and that she would get sweaty palms and a hammering heartbeat when she visited her in-laws. She knew something deeper must be going on when someone new joined her weekly foursome of tennis and she became nervous and self-conscious—two feelings she doesn't normally experience.

Using the meQuilibrium program, Meagan uncovered an iceberg belief that "I must appear competent and in control at all times." Suddenly, all these disparate, apparently unrelated incidents made sense. They were united by the iceberg, which cut a broad swath in her life and turned performance situations into very high stakes.

Up until now in the program, we've been talking only about automatic thoughts and the styles we develop around them. Thought feeds are usually about what's going on right then and there, so they're pretty easy to access. But these thoughts only address what pokes out above the surface, and there's more than meets the eye when it comes to an iceberg. Just because we can't see the hidden parts, though, doesn't mean they're not there. In fact, that's what makes them so hazardous.

The interesting thing about iceberg beliefs is that many of them are double-edged swords. A belief of "I should do everything perfectly" may drive you to work hard and excel—all positives. In the extreme, though, it means your minimal acceptable standard is perfection. Being human, that's impossible to meet. That means your ideal and your real are far apart, and as you know, that results in sadness and shame because you're not meeting your own standards.

To the extent that an iceberg accurately reflects our values and worldview, it can be extremely valuable. Take Joyce, for example. Joyce, fifty-five, is a principal at an inner-city high school. Joyce has an iceberg belief that "Everyone has the potential to succeed if they work hard." This fuels her to be an inspiring educator with the highest graduation rate in her district. That iceberg serves her in that setting.

However, the reality is that any academic performance is a combination of talent and hard work. Some kids just don't have the same level of talent. If one of Joyce's students was not succeeding no matter how much motivation she threw at him or her, then she would likely make judgments about that student (or herself) that might be unfair, such as "This student isn't working hard enough" or "I haven't come up with the right incentive yet," because her iceberg is inaccurate. She is well-meaning, but this belief may cause problems for students who don't match it—or for herself if she doesn't meet her own expectations. Attempting to incentivize improvement in a student who is already doing the best she can by working on motivation when the problem really is poor study habits is a waste of both her time and the student's. There are some circumstances in which her iceberg serves her and some in which it does not.

Some icebergs are not at all useful or even accurate, such as "I must never show my feelings" or "People will always let you down." They might be flat-out wrong, or just outdated. It's normal for a child to develop the belief of "I need to be taken care of at all times," but you can imagine that belief might not lead to the most successful adult relationships.

> **WHEN ICEBERGS COLLIDE:** Have you ever felt pulled hard in two different directions? Inner conflicts are often a result of competing icebergs crashing into each other. For instance, if you hold the belief "I should always be there for my family" along with "I need to excel at everything I do," you can see how easily stress can erupt at 6:00 p.m. when you're expected home for family dinner and you still have a critical deadline to meet. The fact is, iceberg beliefs tend to hold us to impossible standards and, in doing so, make us more stressed. On Day 10, you'll learn how to reroute your icebergs to avoid collisions and achieve balance in your work and personal life.
>
> . . . .

When we bump up against these, the stress fallout can be huge. It can cause clouded thinking, paralysis, panic, anger, and more. If you have an iceberg belief that things should go smoothly, it will really rock your world if you miss that train or don't hit the mark with your work product, and it may lead you to give up on things that are not easy but important, like that diet or exercise program. Like their namesake, iceberg beliefs can be difficult to steer around and can even sink your ship.

By the end of today, you'll know how to easily identify, classify, and navigate around your own iceberg beliefs.

Take Action

Before you can navigate around icebergs (or melt or keep them . . . we'll get to that in a minute), we need to get a handle on what your particular deep-seated beliefs are.

Icebergs come in three different flavors, each of which represents different domains in our lives: achievement, social, and control.

The Three Iceberg Domains

• The Achievement Domain encompasses school, work/career, and official or unofficial roles in our community or organizations. Common achievement icebergs include:

> *"Being successful is what matters most."*
>
> *"Failure is a sign of weakness."*
>
> *"I must never give up."*
>
> *"I should get everything right."*
>
> *"If I can't do something perfectly, I shouldn't do it at all."*
>
> *"I must appear professional at all times."*
>
> *"People should work hard no matter what job they're doing."*
>
> *"I'm meant to be successful/wealthy/influential."*
>
> *"Any child of mine should do well in school/be popular."*

• The Social Domain encompasses the world of relationships, intimate partners, children, in-laws, siblings, extended family members, friends, and social acquaintances. Common social icebergs include:

"It's my job to make sure people are happy."

"I always want people to think the best of me."

"Avoid conflict at all costs."

"You can't trust people."

"I should always be there for the people I love."

"Spouses/significant others should always put their partner first."

- The Control Domain involves how you deal with an erratic world, gain mastery over your life, keep to a regimen or schedule, have things turn out the way you want them to, or feel safe and secure. Common control icebergs include thoughts like:

"Strong people don't ask for help."

"I can't handle messy situations."

"Good things happen to good people; bad things happen to bad people."

"If you want it done right, do it yourself."

"The world should be fair."

"Incompetent people should get out of my way (especially on the road!)."

"People should always be on time."

"I should be allowed to eat/do/buy/wear anything I want."

"Things should work properly."

There are two ways to identify your personal icebergs: The first option is to look over the common icebergs listed on pages 98 and 99 and choose the ones that resonate most for you. Some, because they don't ring true for you, will sound ridiculous and laughable. A person who doesn't have the belief that "Failure is a sign of weakness" will find that idea preposterous. Just skip over those and keep reading. When you find yourself nodding in agreement with one, you'll know you've hit upon one that's true for you.

The second option is to think back to a big, emotional situation that came up for you recently. The more recent, the better. Was your reaction out of proportion to the triggering event? If so, that is your signal that there was a larger thought fueling the greater emotion. Often, the thinking happens so fast that we don't see it. But if we slow the thinking down enough, we can see that there's a thought that's being inserted in there that's taking us off course.

How to Spot an Iceberg

1. Look for the words *must* or *should*. Those are always a good tip-off. Variations of these include *need, have to, supposed to,* and similar phrases.

2. Look for an emotional upheaval that is disproportionate to what the event at hand warrants. If you go ballistic because you spill coffee on your shirt, it's a clue that an iceberg may be lurking beneath the surface (perhaps "I must always show my best side to the world").

Andrew tells a classic story in his workshops about this type of emotional mismatch. It's about a man; let's call him Michael. One night, Michael had to pull an all-nighter to get an emergency project done for a client. He was working in his office upstairs, and his wife was downstairs reading. It was trash night, and in his family, it's his job to take out the trash. Michael heard the trash truck coming down the street, and he knew his wife could hear it, too. He thought, "She knows how crazy busy I am right now. Surely this time she'll take out the trash." A minute later, his wife walked into his office and told him to take out the trash.

Michael did not respond well. He spat out okay to his wife, muttering a curse as she headed back downstairs and resolving not to take the trash out that night—or ever again. He paced up and down in his office like a caged animal, fists clenched and heart pounding, while he felt the red-hot flush of anger rise to his face. It took Michael a good hour or more to get calm enough to resume his work. That was a full hour lost, compared to the five minutes it would have taken him to take the trash out. Not only was Michael robbed of time and focus that night. He was also robbed of grace and resilience.

If you're Michael, the trick is to see and evaluate the event in its most basic form, without editorializing. First, get clear on the facts, and nothing but. What happened, really? In this instance, Michael had to take out the garbage. That's it. Okay. What about you? What's your garbage moment?

Next, evaluate whether the event warranted your level of reaction. At face value, how much of a violation of Michael's rights was this, really? What did having to get up and take out the trash really cost him? Five minutes, tops. On a scale of 1 to 10, maybe this was a violation of a 1 or 2. But his anger level registered somewhere around a 9—clearly a disconnect be-tween the event and the emotional response, which indicates an iceberg had edged its chilly mass into the mix.

Remember the examples at the beginning of this chapter? What happened in Robert's case was that he got a parking ticket. That's the basic fact. Did that warrant a blood-pressure-raising tantrum and a bruised toe from kicking a parking meter? Nalani learned her computer would take six days to fix. That's what happened. Does that jibe with a full-on meltdown and hyperventilating? You see where we're going with this. Obviously there is more going on than what we're seeing at face value, so we need to get to that stuff underneath to unhook ourselves.

How?

Start with what you know—the bold-faced facts of what happened—and try to isolate the thought that was running through your head in that moment. In Michael's case, his wife asked him to take out the trash, and that triggered the thought that this was a violation of lost time.

Drill Down to Detect Icebergs

1. Looking at the facts of what happened, why is that so upsetting to me?

2. What does that (my answer to #1) mean to me?

3. What is the worst part of that (my answer to #2) for me?

4. Assuming my answer to #3 is true, why is that so upsetting to me?

Then, ask yourself the four questions below to drill down. Here's how that played out for Michael:

Question #1: Looking at what happened, why is that so upsetting to me?
Answer: Because she interrupted my work on a crucial project for something trivial.

Question #2: What does that (my answer to #1) mean to me?
Answer: That my wife doesn't respect my work.

Question #3: What is the worst part of that (my answer to #2) for me?
Answer: That she doesn't respect me, because she knows how important my work is to me.

Question #4: And why is that so upsetting to me?
Answer: Because people should support and respect me at all times.

Bingo!
There it was: "People should support and respect me at all times." When we hit upon the word *should*, we know we're there. The trick is to keep drilling down until you get to that absolute, broad-based statement of belief. Notice that now we understand where Michael's big, emotional response came from. A loss of five minutes can't explain anger at a level 9, but having your life partner violate one of your fundamental rules of life (as Michael saw it) does account for a 9 outburst.

By the way, the "Michael" in this story is Andrew. This is an actual event from his life that happened long ago and was the catalyst for much of his work on iceberg beliefs that you're learning today, including his surefire method of navigating around our icebergs once we uncover them.

Now, let's learn how to get around those troublesome icebergs.

There are three ways to deal with an iceberg belief: embrace it, melt it, or steer around it. Which path you choose depends on the usefulness of the iceberg.

EMBRACE THE ICEBERG (WHILE SHAVING OFF THE TROUBLE SPOTS)

Some icebergs reflect what we like about ourselves and want to keep, like "I should always be there for the people I love." Those core values are worth keeping. They can motivate and drive us to excel.

But knowing that all icebergs have a downside, we need to recognize when their sharp edges are causing conflict. For instance, if your aging parents live three thousand miles away, you can't always be there for them. So you have to make room for reality. The trick is to preserve the value belief but shave off the jagged trouble spots.

Let's take a look at this in action. "People should always be on time" is a great iceberg for punctuality, but what happens when you're running late due to unforeseen circumstances? A jack-knifed semi on the highway is outside your control, no matter how early you left to get to that dinner date. When *big* frustration comes up here, it's a signal that your iceberg is floating nearby. It's also the moment to evaluate your iceberg, and if you determine it's one that you want to keep but it *is not serving you in this particular situation*, find a way to not get poked by it. The key is to figure out how to compromise without feeling like you're violating a core value.

In this particular situation, you're coming up against a control iceberg, and in any life, there are limits to what you can and can't control. Sometimes you have to cut yourself some slack and get flexible with your rule. There is literally nothing you can do about the broken-down truck causing the backup, but it's up to you whether you are going to allow the situation to hijack your emotions. Remember, you can't control certain events, but you can change how you respond to them.

Here is where a mantra can come in handy, something you tell yourself when you bump up against your iceberg. With it, you can calmly solve the problem and do the damage control that's needed.

For instance, let's go back to the jack-knifed semi. There you are, at a dead stop, and there's not a thing you can do about it. Grrr! You can continue to fume, but that doesn't get you into effective problem-solving mode. Or, you could take this approach:

"I'm going to be late for that date, and there's nothing I can do about it. I know this is exactly when I bump up against my iceberg about promptness. So, I have a choice: I either slam into the iceberg and get all frustrated and flustered, or I can do something to mitigate the situation. Okay, first thing is to leave voice mails and e-mails on all his devices to head him off. Good. I've done damage control with him, now let me do it with myself.

"What is most upsetting about this for me? That he'll think I'm not the kind of person who's on time. Well, that's ridiculous. You can set your watch by my arrival on ninety-nine out of one hundred occasions. Even with this event, my reputation's intact. Time to cut myself some slack and realize that **I'm only human, and sometimes stuff happens**.*"*

Having a mantra like this enables you to manage the internal conflicts that arise when daily life requires you to get flexible around your core icebergs.

When Our Safety Icebergs Get Rocked

No control iceberg is bigger than the ones we hold around our loved ones' welfare. We are excellent at creating certain parameters in our minds to keep us feeling safe. If we believe that good things happen to good people and bad things only happen to bad people, or that people who take care of themselves don't get sick, then we feel like we have some control. But 9/11 broke that iceberg for many people, and it was very troubling. Suddenly, our ground shifted and we were left thinking, "If it could happen to them, it could happen to me." Our safety signal was gone, but the truth is, all along it was only partially true. We do have some control over our health and our safety, but we don't have full control, because we live within an ecosystem that introduces other factors.

Nothing is perfectly random, and nothing is perfectly controllable. Life has no guarantees, and that's part of this ride. Once we realize where our control ends, we can stop trying to grasp for what's out of our reach and exercise our powers where they are effective. We can let go and let life unfold, leading to a far greater sense of peace.

MELT THE ICEBERG

Often, for icebergs that we form in childhood, the cons far outweigh the pros. For instance, "I should be respected by all people at all times" is just not justified. You can almost hear the stomping of the feet and crossing of the arms of a child. This belief will cause way more pain and frustration than good in your life, so we need to melt that iceberg, or reshape it into one about respect that's more tenable.

Perhaps "I deserve basic respect, but that does not mean that people should grant every wish I have" might serve you better. In that case, it's not a ridiculously wild expectation, and you won't flip out if the mechanic says he can't fix your car until early next week (that is, as long as he is actually repairing your car in the order in which it arrived and/or the order in which he can get the parts). When you're genuinely not getting the respect *to which you're entitled*, then you can take appropriate action.

The key is to come up with a mantra—an "ice breaker"—that you will say to yourself when you crash into your icebergs so that, with practice, you can eventually melt them. Here are a few good examples:

Iceberg Belief: "I should do everything perfectly."
Ice Breaker: "Here I go again, thinking I have to get everything exactly right. No one can do that. I'm not Superwoman. I'm not going to hold myself hostage to that 'museum piece' of an iceberg from my childhood. As an adult, I know that it's good to strive for success, but perfection should never be the goal."

Iceberg Belief: "I need to be taken care of at all times."

Ice Breaker: "There's that old iceberg floating up from my past again. As an adult, I have been looking after myself for years. I've been able to do it before, and I can do it now, too."

Iceberg Belief: "I work hard, so I should be allowed to eat as many treats as I want."

Ice Breaker: "Says who? By what right or entitlement should I be allowed to eat anything I want? Bodies and metabolisms don't always work that way. Mine doesn't, and lots of other people can't get away with that, either. Even those who can eat all the treats they want and not gain weight aren't doing their bodies any good by getting away with it."

STEER AROUND THE ICEBERG

Sometimes, you'll bump up against an iceberg that isn't serving you, but it only shows up in one or two very specific situations. For example, many men have developed the following iceberg: *"A real man can fix anything."* It drives them to don that toolbelt once a year and risk life and limb to fix the air-conditioning unit. When they fail to fix it, they get frustrated and down. They've been found wanting as men! The good news is that they'll only hit this iceberg in these very narrow straits.

Melting big icebergs can be resource-intense, and it doesn't happen right away. Challenge . . . melt . . . challenge . . . melt. It's a process. So you want to choose the ones worth spending your mental energy on. Certain ones may pop up only in specific situations, like, say, when you visit your in-laws. These icebergs are not hitting a broad swath of your life, so they aren't worth the bother of melting. But you do need a map to help steer around them.

Try to think of your situation-specific icebergs and when they might come up, which will enable you to plan ahead for hot spots. Do they happen when you need to fix something around the house, at events at your child's school, on tax day?

Next, think of the steps you can take to minimize their effect in these particular circumstances. Here are a few examples:

Iceberg Belief: "I should be treated with love and respect by my family at all times."

When It Shows Up: When my teenager disobeys me, talks back, or takes out his bad mood on me, I get very angry.

Ice Breaker: "This is just a stage he's going through. He's a teen, so he's testing limits and trying to figure out the world and his place in it. It's part of his development. It's not personal; however, it's my prerogative and my job to hold him to standards and to hold him to rules. Let me wait until things calm down and then let him know what I expect without yelling."

Iceberg Belief: "If someone takes a job, they should do their very best at it (otherwise quit and give it to someone who cares)."

When It Shows Up: When a waiter or waitress gets my order wrong. It drives me nuts.

Ice Breaker: "Getting my order wrong doesn't mean they don't care about doing a good job. This person is working a job that has a lot of moving parts. So perhaps I need to show a little more compassion here. Besides, I came to enjoy the company of my dining companion, not to be the employee police. That's the manager's job, not mine."

Starting today, you can say good-bye to big emotional outbursts and hello to a far greater sense of mastery over your world. Identifying and navigating around your iceberg beliefs has a powerful effect on your ability to do everything from stick to a fitness regimen to achieving harmony in your work/home balance. If you need to take an extra day or two with this skill, by all means do so. It's that important. This gets to the heart of so many issues that cause us stress in life, and steers us into far smoother waters.

Now it's your turn. How will you navigate your icebergs?

My Plan to Navigate Iceberg Beliefs

The core-value icebergs I want to keep long-term but that sometimes cause me conflict are:

What I will say to myself to get around the emotional pull each creates:

My icebergs that are wrong or no longer serve me are:

The ice breakers I will say to myself to melt them are:

My icebergs that show up only occasionally are:

These icebergs tend to show up when:

The steps I will take to minimize their effect on me are:

Day Seven

Banish the Burnout

Q *The Payoff: Greater fulfillment in your everyday life*

Today is a turning point. Today we're going to teach you our proven formula for banishing burnout so that you can wake up and live your days feeling energized, balanced, and—yes—happy.

A major cause of burnout is having more bad events in our days than good. Makes sense, doesn't it? When your days are filled with nothing but blowups at work, time crunches, headaches, and mundane drudge, you're bound to feel fried.

Up until this point in the program, we've been working to solve the problems in your life that are causing you stress and impairing your ability to effectively manage it. You've acquired skills to regulate your stressful

> "If nothing goes wrong in your life, that's great. But that's not real life. Things do go wrong. We lose our keys. Loved ones get sick. Life is messy and it will knock you around. So it's crucial that we load up on the good to boost our resilience."
>
> —Andrew

emotions, rewire faulty thinking, sleep and eat better to sustain your physical resilience, and sharpen your focus. You're putting out fires, quieting the upheavals, and getting yourself to stable, even ground. That's all great.

But remember, we don't want to just get you to feeling "fine." The secret to long-term stress management is to mediate the bad *while also adding in the good*. That's what today is about.

We all have good things that buoy us and give us a healthy boost of self-esteem, like spending quality time with our kids or mentoring someone at work (a proven stress-buster, by the way). And we all have things that pull us down, like missed deadlines, overscheduled days, traffic, problems at home. More bad events, clearly, equal more stress. The more good you stock in your favor, the better you will be able to manage your stress.

We're not going to get to happiness or contentment—or even to a state of lasting anti-stress—just by getting to zero. If you use the negativity-busting skills you're learning in this program, you'll get a lot of improvement. But that only gets us to neutral. We need to dial in to the positives if we want lasting change. Stockpiling the positive (and, as you'll learn tomorrow, strengthening your ability to fully live in it) is your long-term insurance policy for meQuilibrium.

THE SEESAW OF LIFE: Picture a teeter-totter, like one you might see on a playground. On one side are the bad events in your life, and on the other, the good events. If you lift away the bad events, you can sit at the fulcrum and hang out there as long as you like. You're safe at neutral. But life is what it is, and inevitably, another troubling event will come along to land on the negative side and send it teetering back down to the ground—that is, if there's nothing bearing weight on the positive end. If you've loaded up the positive end with good stuff, you have a natural counterbalance working in your favor.

You already know that when it comes to upping your overall ability to handle stress, emotional regulation is top on the list of importance. But coming right up behind it is recalibrating the ratio of good events to bad in your life. Our research has shown that striking that balance is essential for your resilience and overall sense of peace and well-being.

That might seem obvious, but we're not talking about just passively keeping a tally of all that goes on in your days. Notice we didn't say "having" a balance, but "striking" a balance. This is an active skill you can learn. Your days are filled with positives to offset the negatives, and today we're going to show you how to find the ones that are already there as well as how to create new ones.

Today is a day to take a pause and look at the bigger picture. What nourishes you? What depletes you? At meQuilibrium, we refer to the positives as "lifts" and the negatives as "drags." Typical drags include things like conflicts at work, being strapped financially, loneliness, feeling like there aren't enough hours in the day, clutter, having difficulty balancing competing demands, and feeling out of control at home or in your social life. On the flip side, traditional lifts are things like having a network of people who are supportive and caring, a clutter-free environment, enjoying spending time with your family, and having activities and endeavors that are engaging and fulfilling.

To boost your resilience, we're not just going to clean up the bad; we're going to really pay attention to the good. We don't typically do very good accounting on what's happening in our lives. We're not evenhanded in what we pay attention to. As a species, we are much more primed to scan for the bad than for the good. It's a deeply wired survival mechanism. Thousands of years ago, you didn't get taken out of the gene pool if you were blindsided by something good; lions jumping out of the grass were your worry, so that's what you were scanning for. A rainbow on the horizon, however beautiful, wasn't going to save your life. This leads us to magnify the bad and minimize the good, which is a one-way ticket to burnout.

How can you strike a balance between the lifts and drags in your daily life? The plan is to weed through your schedule and formulate an action plan to ditch the drudge that can go, reframe what can't, and load up a little more on the good stuff so that your days can feel more meaningful and enjoyable again.

The Four Corners of Balance

Before we take action, let's look at the four elements that are needed to recalibrate the balance of good and bad events.

The Four Corners of Balance

- Ditch the drudge

- Reframe the required

- Add in the good stuff

- Do active accounting

DITCH THE DRUDGE

Walk the dog. Drive to work. Write your daily report. Sit through a meeting. Make dinner. Pay the bills.

Let's face it: some of life's to-do's aren't that much fun. Sometimes, our schedules are stressful not because of the quantity of events but because of the quality. Day after day filled with the same routine tasks can wear us down and ultimately feel as stressful as pressure-packed ones. We don't want to shirk our long list of responsibilities, and the idea of adding in anything more—even if it's positive and fulfilling—feels even more stressful. So what's a busy person to do?

The answer to that question is to connect to something deeper than what you see on the surface. Hang on—we'll explain.

There are lots of things we all need to do that can feel like a drain. At the top of that list for many people are chores. Going to the supermarket, getting the car washed, paying your bills, organizing the garage or closets . . . all the things we need to do to keep our lives running. These events can, of course, feel like drudgery. Or, if you connect to them in a different way, they can give you a deeper sense of purpose.

For instance, paying bills can be boring and maybe even annoying; but paying your home, insurance, credit card, and tuition bills because it keeps your family's well-being secure casts this chore in a different light. It all comes down to finding the meaning behind the task.

Today we'll parse your daily routine for the activities that feel like a drain to determine what can go, what can be delegated, and what has to stay. Then we'll reframe the required.

> "As a working wife, mother of two, and dedicated career woman, I have learned that *balance* is a myth. But *balancing* might just save my life."
>
> —Jan

REFRAME THE REQUIRED

Some tasks on your drudge list simply can't be cut or delegated; they have to get done. But *why*? That's the key question here.

Often, we believe we have no choice about doing things we don't want to do. But the stark reality is that we always have a choice. We don't *have* to meet our deadlines at work, pick up the dry cleaning, or even pay the bills. It's a free country, and we're adults with free will. Of course, that doesn't mean there won't be consequences. By doing the tasks, we're choosing to not incur those consequences.

Sure, you can choose to blow off the timely request from your boss, but chances are, that won't yield the raise or promotion you might be hoping for. You can choose to not pay your electricity bills, but you'll be stuck sitting in the dark. You can choose to skip doing the laundry, or you can choose to wash your clothes so that you don't show up to work looking (and smelling) unkempt. When you put this issue in the context of choice, you see that it's always up to you. Finding the "why" behind what you choose to do helps you find the value in your actions and lightens any task considerably.

Take going to the grocery store as an example. One way to look at it might be, "I hate this chore. The carts never work right, it's always cold in the supermarket, it's just such a pain to schlepp all this stuff to the car and up the steps into the house. I got my law degree *for this*?!"

Yes, indeed, that sounds like drudge, no doubt about it. But what's the real reason you go to the supermarket? What's the bottom line of what you're doing there? *"I'm grocery shopping to get nutritious food for my family. While this may not be a great adventure, it is a noble deed."* That small shift changes this from a drag into an active, engaged choice.

ADD IN THE GOOD STUFF

What nourishes you? What makes you smile? What gives you that internal lift of joy, contentment, or pride? A little later, you'll identify your personal good stuff and make a plan for easily adding it in.

DO ACTIVE ACCOUNTING

Balancing the good and bad events is an ongoing endeavor. It's something you'll need to do every day, and the way to keep yourself on track is through active accounting.

Deploying this skill in your daily life is startlingly easy. For every bad, irritating, annoying, or aggravating thing that happens, consciously try to create something good to counteract it. Try to keep it in the same domain: home, work, physical, achievement, social, and so on. For instance, if you have a difficult morning with one of your kids, spend some time that day thinking about something positive you can do with them that weekend to balance it out. If you have a setback at work, reach out to someone you've been thinking of getting in touch with to launch an idea that you're excited about. At first, this will take conscious effort, but within just a few days, it will start to become habit.

Take Action

Follow these steps to strike the Four Corners of Balance in your daily life.

Step One: Ditch the Drudge

We're going to start by getting a handle on how you spend your time. At the start of your day today (or tomorrow, if you're reading this in the evening), think through your schedule and to-do list, and identify the activities—big or small—that you hate to do. Your list might look something like this:

My Drudge List

- Call the plumber about the sink that's still leaking
- Call my mother to see how she's feeling

Delegate to De-stress

Does the idea of delegating make you want to slam this book shut and say we just don't understand? Rest assured, we do. Jan has helmed multiple large corporations, and she knows firsthand the pull to do everything herself—as well as the enormous value in trusting your team and delegating.

If delegating causes big emotions to come up for you, use the skill you learned on Day 6 to identify and navigate around your control beliefs (e.g., "I have to do everything myself if I want it done right"). While you're doing that work, here are Jan's favorite tips for effective delegating:

1. Be patient, and give your team or colleagues some time and space.

2. Trust your people, and assume the best will happen until it doesn't.

3. Be ready to redirect when something doesn't go as planned. Remember: *Redirect* does not mean *jump in.*

- Finish the draft of the proposal to give to my client
- Go to the post office to send back the sweater I ordered online
- Make an appointment with the pediatrician to take my son in for a checkup
- Find the paperwork to send to the accountant
- Participate in my weekly conference call with my colleagues
- Clip the dog's nails

Once you have your list, look through and see what things you can reasonably cut or reduce. If they are work related, can you delegate them to someone else or ask a colleague to help with some of the load? If they are household chores, can you ask your partner to take up the slack or enlist your children to share in the responsibilities? If possible, choose one or two that you can eject from your schedule. If it's not possible, keep reading; the next step, "Reframe the Required," is for you.

Step Two: Reframe the Required
For those activities that you categorize as boring, annoying, or otherwise unpleasant but need to keep, reframing will greatly lighten the burden. You want to look for the meaning behind the activity. Why are you doing it? What's the greater purpose? Go through your list, and reframe each one. Here are a few examples that might help you reframe your drudge activities:

> *"I'm at work to make money to support my children. While this specific task isn't important, the greater goal is."*

> *"I don't love walking the dog in the rain or clipping his nails, but I do love my dog. He brings me a lot of joy, and caring for him keeps him healthy."*

"I know I will sit on hold for thirty minutes with the cable company, but the big game is on Sunday, and I want my boyfriend to be able to watch it. This is one small way I can make him happy, and that makes me happy."

"Paying the bills is how I make sure we have electricity, heat, and phone service in our house. It is part of what keeps our home running smoothly. When my kids sleep under this blanket of security I provide, it makes me feel good."

"This project may feel like a slog, but it will make a big impression on my client and likely lead to more referrals and income. I will also feel a great sense of accomplishment when it is done, and that's always a boost for me."

"I'm going to the gym so that I can be healthy for myself and my family. Working out gives me more energy and helps me think better. Plus, exercise keeps me looking good, and that feels great!"

Step Three: Add in the Good Stuff

We're not quite done parsing your to-do list. Now go through your upcoming schedule and to-do list, and identify the activities that feel engaging, fun, or even quietly rewarding. No pleasure is too small. You're looking for anything in your upcoming day that gives you a little spark. For example:

My Good Stuff

- Taking my morning yoga class
- Calling my friend Stephanie to hear how her trip to Paris was

- Wearing my new black boots
- Presenting my big sale at this week's staff meeting
- Enjoying the dinner my husband said he is going to make
- Snuggling with my kids while we watch television
- Reading my book before bed

Read through your Good Stuff list and really take a moment to absorb how those events make you feel. It's an instant lift, isn't it? Looking ahead, each day be sure to schedule at least three or more good events into your day. Remember, they don't have to be big events; anything that makes you smile or boosts your sense of pride, accomplishment, joy, or meaning will do the trick. Even if you can't add three every day, make sure to add at least three enjoyable activities to each week—and to ensure they stay there week after week, month after month.

> **MAKE TIME FOR BEAUTY AND HUMOR:** Surrounding yourself with beauty can cut through the bleakest of the bleak.
> Those who are most resilient literally schedule beauty and humor into their days rather than just wait for these sources of joy to come to them. So, commit to watching Comedy Central for thirty minutes each day, or actively set aside time to flip through the pages of your favorite photography book or listen to a piece of uplifting music. Whatever speaks to you will help you through.

If your reaction to reading this is, "That sounds great, but I don't have the time for that," it's a clue that you're hitting an iceberg. Remember, they can do a number on our ability to change our habits—and you are, in fact, here to change. One of the most common ones that comes up around this is, "Busy people don't have time for fun." Is this iceberg useful to you?

Is it one that needs to be melted, steered around, or embraced while shaving off the rough edges? Do a little digging using the skills you learned on Day 6 to see what might be getting in the way of injecting more positives into your life.

Step Four: Do Active Accounting
Spend a few minutes making a list of everything challenging that happened to you today—big, small, it doesn't matter. Then, for each one, think of something you could do (within the same domain) to offset it. For instance:

My Challenge: A rough morning arguing with my husband while we were rushing to get the kids off to school and ourselves to work on time.
My Plan to Offset It: Call or e-mail during the day to let him know something I appreciate that he does to keep our family life running smoothly.

My Challenge: Hearing from my client that she wasn't happy with what I had delivered.
My Plan to Offset It: Spend time with the client discussing what's missing and how to fix it. Then read an e-mail from a highly satisfied client to remind myself that I'm good at what I do.

Keep doing this, and within a few days, you'll start to train yourself to add in a positive boost each and every time a negative comes along.

Once you ditch some drudgery, reframe what remains, and inject some fun into your life, you'll start to have more positive feelings about even the most boring tasks. You'll feel more fulfilled, and that's a giant step in the right direction away from stress and into meQuilibrium.

My Plan to Banish Burnout

I choose to work on this skill because:

The activities on my Drudge list that I can ditch are:

The activities on my Drudge list that I can delegate are:

My immediate plan for delegating those is:

The activities on my required list that need to remain are:

When the dread of doing them comes up, I will reframe each one as follows:

The three good things I will add into my day tomorrow are:

Here is specifically how and when I will do those things:

Here are the icebergs that come up for me when I take time to add in good stuff:

Here is how I will navigate around those icebergs:

My plan to offset challenges that I foresee coming is:

Day Eight

Tune Your Positive Radars

 The Payoff: A deeper wellspring of positive emotions to sustain you through challenges

Yesterday, you learned about balancing the proportion of good to bad events in your life, and that's a fantastic start. We do need to load up on good things, but there's a second—and equally important—component to this. We also have to *actively train ourselves to look for positive emotions and take advantage of them when they are here.* In other words, we need to appreciate our emotional response to the good stuff fully to get the real and lasting benefits. Today, you're going to learn how to tune in to positive emotions and live in them fully.

> "Love, contentment, pride, joy, appreciation of beauty . . . these are the neglected cousins of stress management."
>
> —Andrew

Some people, no matter how loaded up they are on the good stuff, take lemonade and turn it back into lemons. They're missing out on the benefits. We've done a good job of trying to amp up the amount of positive events in your life, but are you really, fully appreciating them when they happen? We want to make sure that when the positives do come up, your radar is as set to ping on those as it is focused on the bad stuff. Today we're going to clear the mental cobwebs so that you can get the full benefit of the good stuff you have (and are adding) in your life.

Our Positive Radars

When Andrew conducts a workshop, he asks by a show of hands, "How many of you have been overwhelmed sometime in the past week by frustration, anxiety, anger, or whatever your pet negative emotion is?" Nearly every hand in the room goes up.

Then he asks, "Now, when's the last time you were overwhelmed by contentment?"

Crickets.

Sadly, we don't take our positive emotions as seriously as the negative ones, so they tend to fly under the radar. We don't notice contentment, because there's no survival value in noticing that we have everything we need. Remember, as humans, we're not evenhanded in what we pay attention to emotionally. We're hardwired to scan for the bad and overlook the good. It's an ancient survival mechanism. We've long since outgrown the usefulness of that imbalance, and yet we haven't shed the habit. We focus determinedly on what's wrong in our lives, but how often do we get into our cars and say, "Wow, thank goodness—a full tank of gas!"? We notice when we're out of time, but do we ever notice when we have enough? We're scanning for the dearth rather than the plenty.

The problem with that is that many of us are living in a scorching desert of stress. The sands are encroaching more and more, taking the pleasure out of each day. These moments of contentment, joy, enthusiasm, and love are a lush oasis. Yet most of us, when we come across one of these mini-paradises, pause long enough just to nibble at a date or two, take a swig out of a coconut, and go along our busy way. We forget (or don't make time) to indulge in this bounty of plenty.

When contentment comes along, we need to do more than nibble and run. We need to feel how it changes our physiology; how it relaxes our tense muscles, slows our heart rate and breathing, sends a warm flush of peace and tranquility through our entire being. We don't tend to have this full experience of the positive—but it's a skill we can develop.

The way we do that is by developing our inner radars for the positive emotions and fine-tuning them so that we're primed to look for and absorb positive moments. This is the secret to how we recharge.

Take Action

The first action tool here is a skill that some of you may have been using, if maximizing and minimizing is a thinking trap you tend to fall into. It's highly effective for recalibrating your radar toward the positive, and today we're going to suggest it for everyone.

Here's how it works; we've discussed this exercise before, so it should be familiar to you:

At the end of the day today, write down three good things that happened to you. Even on the worst days you can find three good things. They don't have to be earth-shattering events. Finding out your purchase offer on your dream house was accepted is a great addition to the list, but small things like your kid giving you an extra squeeze and unexpectedly saying he loves you count, too. Tomorrow, before you make breakfast, check e-mail, go to the gym, or do anything else, read those three things. Read them, and then go about your business.

At the end of tomorrow, do the same thing. Write down three more good things that happened to you, adding them to your list. The next morning, read those six things. Do this exercise for ten days, and by the end, you'll have thirty good things written down. You will very quickly find that by seeking out the good, you become more attuned to it. You are literally reprogramming your brain to scan for the good stuff.

This is an excellent tool for overall positive conditioning. You can take this a step farther, though, and actually cultivate specific positive emotions you want to experience more of.

Just as Andrew and his research colleagues mapped out the Big 7 negative emotions that get in our way and the negative radars that lead to them, his work has uncovered the Big 6 positive emotions that people seek and the thought radars that garner them. The Big 6 are happiness, pride, interest/engagement, esteem/respect, love, and contentment. We can learn to scan for the good just as capably as we scan for the bad.

Emotions, as we know, are caused by thoughts. Just as frustration is caused by thoughts of not having enough resources, contentment is generated by thoughts of having everything you need. Like negative emotions, positive emotions each come with telltale physical signs to help you recognize them.

When we experience negative emotions, it's easy to feel the full impact on our bodies, minds, and behaviors. We can identify the familiar weight of sadness bearing down or the tears stinging the back of our eyes. We zero right in on intense sensations of anger and so easily tune in to thoughts of impending future threat that we can't do anything but feel anxious.

The opposite is true of positive emotions. When we feel

happiness or pride, we're not as acutely aware of the feelings, and they can waft away if we're not consciously capturing them. We have to focus and deliberately find the thoughts that generate these positive emotions. It's important to practice the skill of focusing on our assets and create awareness of the way positive emotions feel in our bodies.

You can train yourself to develop positive radars to tap into and live these good feelings fully. While we want all of the Big 6 positive emotions in our lives, choose the one that you most want to cultivate more of right now, and follow the steps below to set your radar in that direction. Stick to one, and make it a positive habit before you return for another.

EMOTION	HOW IT FEELS	FUELING THOUGHT
Happiness	Breathing is deeper, slower, and more regular; muscles are relaxed; a smile may cross your face. Your mind may feel like it has a soothing "hum" or "glow." You may become more playful or want to push your limits and be more creative.	"All is great."
Pride	A flush of warmth; an energized mind and body. You experience a desire to do more or achieve more good things.	"I did a good job/did the right thing/behaved admirably."
Interest and engagement	Senses are heightened and keen; breathing is quickened but regular; you may feel as if you have little currents of electricity moving through your body. Your thoughts are racing, not with anxiety but with a creative bounce from one idea to the next. Your eyes widen and you shift forward in your seat or stance.	"This task is just within my capabilities."
Esteem and respect	A warm glow when you're around others who think well of you; breathing is slow and regular. Your mind is clear and sharp, and you feel confident to take on new challenges.	"People think well of me."
Love	A warm glow when you're around those to whom you feel connected and committed; breathing and heartbeat are slow and regular. Your mind has a gentle buzz or hum, and you feel a pull to be with this person you love or who loves you.	"I feel connected and committed to you."
Contentment	Breathing is deeper, slower, and more regular; muscles are relaxed; a smile may cross your face. Your mind may feel like it has a soothing hum or glow; you'll find you want to linger wherever you are.	"I have everything I need."

TUNE YOUR HAPPINESS RADAR

Happiness is triggered by the thought that things are going wonderfully. To increase the frequency of this emotion, you need to reorient your thinking to focus on what's going well in your life, for what you have rather than what you don't.

Scan for Happiness

1. Start with your positive intention. Say, "I want to feel more happiness. That means I need to focus on what's going well in my life rather than on what's not."

2. Make a list of everything good in your life. What's going well? Explore every area of your life, and aim for as broad and long a list as possible. What success have you had at work? What's going well at home or with your kids at school? What is positive about your relationship with your significant other? What's going well with your health or the health of your loved ones? Carry this list with you during the week so that whenever you want to access more happiness, you can easily read it.

3. Live the happiness fully. Get to know your personal happiness sensations; just as with negative emotions, early detection is key. When you notice you're feeling happy, pause and really take in how it feels in your body and in your mind. What are the positives showing up in your behavior? Think of this as imprinting the sensations on your emotional memory. Whatever you're feeling in a happy moment, experience it with all your senses and savor it!

TUNE YOUR PRIDE RADAR

Pride is triggered by the thought that we have done well in the world or lived up to our own standards. To increase the frequency of this emotion, you need to focus on when you've done the right thing, the good thing, the moral thing. It takes practice: we tend to scan more for those times when we took the easy way, let someone down, or failed at a task rather than when we came through or succeeded.

Scan for Pride

1. Start with your positive intention. Say to yourself, "I want to feel more pride. That means I need to focus on what I've done well and the times I met or exceeded my own standards rather than on when I made bad choices."

2. Make a list of when you meet or exceed your own standards, do something well, or do the right thing. Explore every part of your life. How are you doing well at work? When do you do the right thing as a parent, friend, or member of your community? At what do you excel in life? What have you accomplished in your health or fitness goals that you feel good about? Carry this list with you during the week so that whenever you want to access more pride, you can easily read it.

3. Plan for pride. Ask yourself, "What is one thing I can do to generate more pride today?" Perhaps you can complete a project that you've been working hard on or volunteer to help a friend in need. Then follow through on that one thing for an extra dose of pride.

> 4. Live the pride fully. Get to know your personal
> pride sensations. When you notice you're feeling
> pride, pause and really take in how it feels. What's
> going on in your body? How does your mind feel?
> What are the positives showing up in your behav-
> ior? Whatever you're feeling in a moment of pride,
> experience it with all your senses and savor it.

The Power of Pride

Here's how meQuilibrium member Julie, thirty-eight, honed
her pride radar and what that yielded:

*"I have pretty exacting standards for myself when it comes to
my job and being a mom. I demand a lot of myself, and over
the years, that has really gotten me down, because I feel like I
fall short of the mark—a lot. I immediately identified pride as
an emotion I wanted to feel more of, and tried to give myself a
boost there by looking for what I do well instead of what I think
I mess up and feel badly about.*

*"At the end of each day, I took thirty minutes to write in
my journal. I'd list all the times that day when I had met my
own expectations, did something well, or did the right thing.
In the beginning, it was hard. I was so used to finding the negative. But it gradually got easier. Instead of just focusing on
the one thing my boss said I did wrong in the project, I'd write
down the things she said I did well. I'd take note of the times
I found time for a workout or to read to my son even when I
was dog-tired. I used to just take that stuff for granted. But
not anymore.*

"It has been six months since I started doing this. I don't do

it every day anymore—probably more like once a week. But whenever I find myself feeling shame, I stop to find the things I did well and the times I did the right thing. I enjoy the pride!"

TUNE YOUR INTEREST AND ENGAGEMENT RADAR

Interest/engagement is the polar opposite of boredom, lethargy, or just feeling "blah." It's triggered when a task is just within our capabilities to achieve. To increase the frequency of that positive emotion, you need to reorient your thinking and train yourself to focus on times when you feel the spark of being fully invested in or lit up by something.

Scan for Interest and Engagement

1. Start with your positive intention. Say to yourself, "I want to feel more interest and engagement. That means I need to focus on when I find things more stimulating, rather than on my boredom."

2. Make a list of when you are typically most engaged and interested. Is it when you are in the company of certain people? When you are exploring something new on your own? When you are in the flow of your work? What activities make you feel the most energized and engaged?

3. Plan for interest and engagement. Ask yourself, "What's one thing I can do today that will capture my interest and engagement?" It can be something as small as seeing a movie you've been hearing great buzz about or as ambitious as going skydiving.

4. Live the interest and engagement fully. Get to know what it feels like, in your body and mind, to be interested and engaged. When you notice you're feeling that spark of engagement, pause and really take it in. How are you behaving? Are you talking a little faster, breathing a little more quickly, leaning in? Is your mind buzzing with ideas? Whatever you're feeling in a moment of interest and engagement, take note with all your senses and enjoy it.

Make It Interesting

Some tasks are inherently boring, and there isn't a lot we can do to dress them up. But here are two tips to spruce them up a little:

1. Play games against yourself. The next time you're doing a mindless task, time yourself. Then the next time you're faced with that chore, try to beat that time. Mihaly Csikszentmihalyi, the psychologist who most studied "flow" (those moments when we're so engrossed that time seems to stand still), showed that assembly-line workers who tried to process the most units in a shift or commit the fewest errors were happiest.

2. Look for the bigger purpose. Here's when your skill of reframing the drudge from Day 7 will come in very handy. Okay, so the task may be mindless, but that doesn't mean it's meaningless. Washing, drying, and folding clothes isn't challenging, and there isn't that much to be interested in or engaged with, but it serves an important pur-

pose. It keeps our families clean and safe. The endless paperwork at the office isn't fun, but it's part of the job that provides us with the money to protect our children. For every boring task, dig a little deeper and identify *why* you do it, and your engagement level in the activity will very likely shift.

TUNE YOUR ESTEEM AND RESPECT RADAR

Esteem and respect are triggered by the thought that people think well of us. To increase the frequency of this emotion, you need to reorient your thinking so that you actively scan for the compliments, accolades, or appreciation you've received.

Scan for Esteem and Respect

1. Start with your positive intention. Say to yourself, "I want to feel more esteem and respect. That means I need to focus on times when others think well of me rather than on when I'm embarrassed."

2. Make a list of when/by whom/where you have felt respected and esteemed. What do your spouse, significant other, friends, and children admire about you? When have your boss or colleagues complimented you? Where in your community are you held in high regard? Carry this list with you, and pull it out whenever you want to feel more respect and esteem. Those reminders will be an instant boost.

3. Fully live the esteem and respect. Get to know what it feels like, in your body and mind, to feel esteem and respect. When you notice you're feeling that lift of esteem and respect, pause and really take it in. Do you feel a warm glow? Do your intellectual abilities feel clear and sharp? Are you inspired to take on new challenges? Take note with all your senses, and let it infuse you.

TUNE YOUR LOVE RADAR

Who doesn't want to feel more love in their life? Love is . . . well, you can fill that in for yourself with your own personal definition. The common denominator for all of us, though, is that love is a positive force.

Love is triggered when we feel connected and committed to another person. To increase the frequency of this emotion, you need to reorient your thinking so that you focus on the enjoyable connections you have with others and your commitment to them.

Scan for Love

1. Start with your positive intention. Say to yourself, "I want to feel more love. That means I need to focus on the connections I have with others and my commitment to them rather than on when I feel lonely."

2. Make a list of the important people in your life and your commitment to them. Explore all the central relationships in your life—romantic relationships, family, children, friends. In what ways are these people special to you? What is unique about each relationship? What is your history with them? The longer the history, the greater the chance for connection.

3. Live the love fully. When you notice you're feeling love, do you feel a warm glow or a gentle buzz in your mind? Do you feel a pull to be with the people to whom you feel connected and committed? Are you inspired to be generous or affectionate? Whatever you're feeling in a love-enriched moment, experience it with all your senses and savor it.

Love and Partnership

It's very easy to take love for granted. For many in long-term relationships, it becomes the backdrop of their lives rather than center stage where it belongs. Here's how Robert was able to use his love radar skill to enhance his feelings of love for his life partner:

"Jenny and I have been together for a lot of years. As time goes by, you tend to forget many of the reasons you got together. You're living in each other's pockets, up close and personal with the other person's bad habits. You're raising kids together and trying to get by financially. Your relationship seems to get worn down over time—or, at least, you start to take things for granted. At least that's what happened to us.

"Lately, I started to make a list of all the reasons I want to be with Jenny. I made notes about all the things we've been through together and all the things we still hope to achieve together in life. Some days get off to a bad start. We're both rushing to work and to get the kids off to school, and we're either arguing or ignoring each other. So, on my way to work, I'll just read through that list and give her a call just to say I love her. I've found it has made me happier. I feel more connected to her, and I find myself looking forward to getting back together at the end of the day. I know it has made her feel more connected, too."

TUNE YOUR CONTENTMENT RADAR

For many years, whenever Andrew asked people what emotion they would like to feel more of, the answer was either love or happiness. But starting around 2008, when the recession hit and the social upheavals occurred as a result (as we were being financially squeezed, being asked to do more with less, and generally just trying to cope with the fast pace and demands of modern life), he began to notice that the answer had changed. People weren't necessarily aiming for happiness. They were looking for contentment.

While happiness and contentment might seem like one and the same thing, they're not. Happiness is about gain—getting something we want that brings us joy, often at a moment or in a place we didn't expect. Contentment is more about having our needs satisfied. If happiness is a wild, exuberant ride, contentment is a peaceful, quieter stroll. Because happiness is a more profound emotion, it has a bigger physiological impact, so it's easier to detect. Contentment is more subtle, so we have to look a little harder to recognize it. It takes practice to recalibrate and find the quieter feelings of contentment in our bodies. Once you've identified your moments of contentment, it's especially important to live in them fully so that they eventually speak to you as loudly as their bigger sibling happiness does.

Contentment is triggered by the thought that we have everything we need to solve problems and enjoy everyday life. To increase the frequency of contentment, you need to train yourself to focus on the strengths, tools, and assets that you do have rather than on the resources you don't.

Scan for Contentment

....

1. Start with your positive intention. Say to your-self, "I want to feel more contentment. That means I need to focus on what I do have at my disposal to achieve my goals rather than on what I don't have."

2. Make a list of your goals and resources. This list has two parts. For the first, list everything you hope to achieve right now, both big and small. It may be a problem that needs solving or a project that needs to get done. Perhaps it's a career goal or even a relationship or social goal. Next, for each one of those goals, ask yourself, "What do I have at my disposal that can help me achieve this goal or solve this problem?" As you make your list, explore every one of your assets, and aim for as big a list as possible. What internal strengths do you have to solve this problem or achieve this goal (e.g., courage, sense of humor, brains, persever-ance)? What material resources do you have to get there (e.g., a budget, materials, tools, time)? What human resources do you have (e.g., personnel, ad-visors, networks, friends, family)? Carry this list with you to read whenever you're feeling frus-trated, to recalibrate toward contentment.

3. Live the contentment fully. Contentment is elu-sive, so when it does come along, it's especially im-portant to pay attention. When you notice you're feeling content, pause and really take in how it feels. Do you feel a warm glow or a pleasant, gen-tle hum in your mind? Is your breathing even

and regular? Do you feel drawn to linger where you are? Whatever you're feeling in a contented moment, experience it with all your senses and savor it.

A Contentment Radar in Action

Here's how meQuilibrium member Faith, forty-four, was able to boost her contentment:

> *"When I'm trying to squeeze in a trip to the supermarket between the end of the workday and picking up the kids, my brain is usually screaming with thoughts like, 'I'm not going to make it in time to pick up my son, I left too late, there aren't enough parking spaces outside the store, I don't think I have enough money for these groceries.' When I have these thoughts, I'm very aware of the frustration that comes up for me. Basically, I freak out.*
>
> *"So now I also try to scan my thoughts when I'm not rushed. The other day, I had an hour before my next appointment and I went to pick up a few items from the supermarket. As I was driving, I listened hard to tune in to my contentment thoughts: 'I've got plenty of time, I've got a car, I've got enough money— I'm good to go.' I now do this regularly and try to enjoy the contentment I feel in those moments as much as I live in the frustration when it's there."*

Trap, Map, and Zap the Negative Intruders

Your final step for honing your positivity radars is to be on the lookout for negative intruding thoughts. Negative thoughts are sneaky; they'll try to worm their way in! If you notice feelings of sadness, guilt, embarrassment, or any of the other Big 7 creeping in while you're tuning to positive, it's a signal that negative thought feeds are running amok and need to be zapped. Pay attention to your body signals (the heaviness of sadness, the red flush of anger) to catch when your pet emotions show up. Building on positivity is too important to let pesky negative thoughts get in your way.

This skill of tuning your positive radar works quickly, and as you practice it, you'll very soon see your overall outlook shift. We really *can* train ourselves to be happier, more engaged, and interested in life; we can experience more good feelings of esteem, love, pride, and contentment. All it takes are the tools and practice. Now you have the tools. The rest is up to you.

My Plan to Tune My Positive Radars

I choose to work on this skill because:

The emotion I would like to experience more of is:

The intention I will set to scan for this emotion is:

This emotion feels like this in my body and mind:

When this emotion arises, here is how I will live it fully:

Day Nine

Find Your Fitness Fault Lines

The Payoff: Motivation, energy, and the pride of sticking with a fitness regimen

Imagine to the east are your fitness goals, and to the west is your busy everyday life. And right down the middle is a giant fault line. What happens to your intentions when the ground beneath you rumbles? The fault line splits open, and your good intentions go tumbling down into oblivion.

The daily upheaval of modern life makes it challenging to fit in exercise, even though we're likely well aware of its benefits— the increased energy; the boost of feel-good brain chemicals, stamina, and strength; and more. The hard part usually isn't knowing what to do; it's getting ourselves to do it. We're too busy, too tired, or we've tried before and haven't stuck with it. For some, even *thinking* about trying to fit in exercise is enough to make them feel anxious or overwhelmed.

> "Movement should be something that de-stresses you, not acts as a source of frustration or discomfort."
>
> —Adam

Today you'll discover how to take the stress out of exercise. We're going to help you find the triggers that cause your fault lines to open and swallow up your time and intentions. We want you to tap into the wellspring of mental sharpness, emotional calm, and physical vibrancy that comes from exercising—*without* stressing about it.

> **NO TIME TO EXERCISE? YOU'RE NOT ALONE**: If you have trouble finding the time or motivation to exercise, or don't always enjoy doing it, you're in good company. A recent Gallup poll showed that about half of American adults find it difficult to exercise regularly. The good news is that meQuilibrium members showed a significant increase in motivation and success after going through the program. Across the board, we saw a 16 percent improvement in the ability to stay with a fitness program. And when we focused on those who started off scoring below the norm on their physical exercise regimen, we saw an 87 percent improvement in the frequency and quality of their workout. So keep reading!

What It Takes

To work, a fitness plan has to have two components: physical and mental. Often people focus only on the physical and throw themselves into a program, but just having the how-to information isn't enough. If it were, we'd all be exercising with ease and frequency! You need both to make and to stick to a plan that will get you where you want to be.

The physical component is the obvious part. You need to literally move your body. We'll give you Dr. Adam's prescription for getting fit and for finding the exercise that's best for you.

On a deeper level, we need to root out the thoughts that might be getting in your way. Fitness hits big emotional buttons, and whenever there are big emotions, we know there are big beliefs lurking. Because iceberg beliefs are our most fundamental values and can represent our deepest fears, it's not surprising that they can derail our best efforts to make healthy lifestyle changes. The reason you may not have succeeded in the past isn't because you haven't tried your best to exercise; it's because you didn't address the underlying beliefs that were silently sabotaging your efforts. You may be unknowingly carrying around some clunkers that are impeding your fitness intentions and efforts.

Where there are icebergs, there are negative thoughts. And where there are negative thoughts, there are roadblocks. We'll highlight the common fitness icebergs to help you isolate yours, and arm you with thought zappers to counteract even the most pernicious of mental intruders that could impede your fitness success.

Excuse or Iceberg?

Negative icebergs get in the way of making good decisions. Because of them, we develop tricky ways of convincing ourselves that we're avoiding something challenging or inconvenient for rational reasons. This is especially true with food, rest, and, of course, exercise. Here's an example from Jan's life of how she can talk herself out of a good choice:

> *"Weekday mornings offer half an hour of family time before we all scatter for work and school. I often struggle to leave the house and go for a run. I have to choose between getting in a quick but invigorating workout and being in the kitchen while the kids have breakfast, a precious window of time together. I know on one level that I'll feel better all day (and be more productive and make better food choices) if I go for the run, but I rationalize not going by telling myself that it is important to be there for the kids; as a working mother, I feel like being present*

*for my family is more valuable than the benefits I'll gain from
the run."*

Who doesn't occasionally look for a reason to blow off exercise? But in this instance, Jan was coming up against a very real internal struggle between serving her family and serving herself. More often than not, she would skip the run and feel the consequences of doing so, perhaps in the form of bad food choices, restlessness in her desk chair, or an inability to fall asleep at night.

In that moment of internal negotiation in which we weigh our two options, if we are aware of our icebergs, we have the ability to step outside the situation and examine the trade-off we've formulated. We can stop and redirect our actions, according to our adult, reasoned thinking, rather than having them unconsciously driven by outdated or unuseful beliefs we formulated long ago.

By the way, in case you missed it, the key phrase in the promise above is *if we are aware of our icebergs*. We can make all the resolutions and sign up for all the fabulously fun fitness classes we want, but unless we consciously direct our choices, we'll end up back where we started, with a lapsed gym membership (and likely a heap of guilt and shame to go along with it).

Take Action

Okay, let's put together your plan. We'll do this in three tiny steps, removing the impediments first before anything else:

1. Navigate the icebergs
2. Challenge the thoughts
3. Get moving

NAVIGATE THE ICEBERGS

Begin by isolating your personal icebergs. Below you'll find some of the most common ones that come up around fitness. Some of these are about our capabilities or capacities, some are beliefs about how we should be spending our time, and some go to the heart of our identity and how we see ourselves.

As you read through them, breeze past the ones that seem wrong or even ridiculous to you—those don't apply to you. When you read one that makes you nod with familiarity and say, "Yes, of course that's so," you'll know you've hit one.

Once you've identified your fitness icebergs, look at them carefully and determine whether they should be melted, steered around, or embraced/shaved. Remember, an iceberg that is wholly outdated and doesn't serve us gets melted, the ones that crop up only in a narrow set of circumstances get steered around, and the ones that represent values we want to keep but are creating problems for us get embraced while we handle the conflict they are generating.

So, for instance, let's say you have the iceberg of "Life isn't supposed to be hard." Chances are, this belief cuts a broad swath in your life and shows up not just around fitness but in your work life, or with anything that presents a challenge. It's pretty damaging, because it really puts a crimp on your reaching out and taking on new opportunities, so it's one that deserves to be melted.

Here, you might challenge and, over time, melt that iceberg by saying something like the following when it shows up: "Anything worth doing is going to require effort. Effort does not equal 'bad.' No one on the planet has ever gotten fit without effort, so why should I? Yes, it feels like work, but the sense

Common Fitness Icebergs

"We don't do exercise in my family/my community/ my culture."

"Being fit just isn't who I am."

"I should be there for my family at all times."

"If I don't do something perfectly, I shouldn't do it at all."

"Things shouldn't feel too hard. If they do, they're not worth doing."

"I don't deserve to have a better life."

"If I get in shape and my partner doesn't, it will drive a wedge between us."

of achievement I will feel at the end will well and truly over-whelm any negative feelings I might have along the way."

Some icebergs are situational and pop up only in the realm of fitness. Because they don't cut such a broad swath in your life, we're not going to bother asserting the mental energy to melt them; we're just going to steer around them. A great example of this type of iceberg is "Being fit just isn't who I am."

A way to steer around it is by challenging that belief's origins. You might say something to yourself like, "Fitness is not who my parents were, and I learned that message early on from them. But that message from way back then has no control over my destiny now. Fitness may not be who I was, but it's who I want to become. As an adult, I'm different from my parents in many ways, so why not in this way, too? It's not a disrespectful thing to live my life differently and to be fit."

Even though you're not tackling this iceberg head-on, if you continue to work out and eat healthfully, then gradually that iceberg will melt all by itself. You'll wake up one day and realize, "Hey, you know what? Being fit *is* who I am." You're in shape, looking and feeling good, and being confronted by so much evidence that your iceberg has no choice but to adjust to your new reality.

For the last example, let's go back to Jan's story. Let's say, like her (and many other working moms), you have an iceberg of "I should be there at all times for my family." That's a wonderful and noble principle, and one worth keeping. The devil here is in the details. What you want to do is hold the belief, but define very concretely what it truly means in the context of your life. If you believe that you should always be there for the people you love, then doesn't that mean something about preserving your health and life span? Spending twenty minutes at the gym three days a week (and away from your kids) to add ten years to your life might just be worth it! Taking care of yourself means not only that you'll be here longer on the planet but that while here you'll be more vibrant, more energetic, more present with them. You're not violating your belief by carving out time for yourself. You're just shaving off the trouble spots that snag you when you bump up against them.

Here's where you need a mantra. You can use something like this: "Sometimes, being there for the people I love means taking care of myself by exercising" or "My needs are not in conflict with my kids' needs. They value my company but will be best served by a parent who is energetic and balanced, not mad at herself for skipping her workout."

If we teach ourselves to stop and think more critically in moments of decision, we have a chance to prevent the stress that comes from making bad choices and gain the resilience that comes from successfully navigating our trouble spots.

CHALLENGE THE THOUGHTS

As you know, negative thoughts—especially the ones that are lifelong habits—have a way of creeping in just when we're making progress on our goals. So let's be ready for them. Here are a few ideas for zapping them.

Thought: "This is too hard."
Thought Zapper: "Yes, this is hard, but it's not *too* hard. Exercise is meant to be challenging, and I am up for the challenge."

Thought: "I couldn't finish (or keep up with) the class/DVD/ workout routine. That proves I'm not cut out for this."
Thought Zapper: "Nonsense. I'm human. Sometimes I'm up for the full workout, and sometimes I'm not. It's a process of getting fit, and I get stronger with each workout."

Thought: "This is boring."
Thought Zapper: "I'm not looking at this the right way. What's my reason for exercising? Is it to be entertained or to get fit? I need to remember my motivating factor, and that will help me reframe this."

Thought: "I'm going to look stupid (or fat . . . or old . . . or ugly . . .)"
Thought Zapper: "Everyone is a beginner at one time or another. No one is looking at me; they are more concerned with

their own workouts. Besides, it's a learning curve, and every time I work out, I get more confident."

What negative thoughts pop up for you when you're exercising or trying to get yourself to do so? What zappers can you apply in those moments to blast them and keep yourself on track?

GET MOVING

Now that you've got your mind aligned with your intentions, let's get you moving!

The fitness advice available to us could paper the planet. The trick is to discover simple guidelines that make it easy for you to find the right path for yourself and to stick with it. Less is more, in that if you can ingrain only the smartest fundamental choices into your thinking, you can make it very easy for yourself. Dr. Adam's guidelines below take the best of world-class thinking and boil it down, giving you the essential formula you need to succeed.

Your task for today is to craft your game plan. Take some time tonight to write this out. The more precise you are, the better your aim—and the better your chances of hitting your target of making fitness a regular part of your life.

Dr. Adam's Exercise Prescription

- Schedule it. Carve out dedicated time for it, just like anything else that's important.

- Make it regular. Although it's ideal to try to do something on most days, on average, three days a week for thirty minutes each time is the minimum most people need to stay healthy and reduce stress. We get increased benefits for every additional day we add in, up to six days each week.

- Make it fit your life. Choose something that is challenging but doable and that fits into your schedule and budget.

- Make it effective. Look for exercise methods that deliver a combination of strength, stretching, and stamina. That might mean weight training, yoga, and some sort of aerobic activity.

- Be realistic. The biggest mistake is to attempt to run a half marathon the first time out, even if that's something you were able to do years ago. If you bite off more than you can chew, you may get discouraged—and could even do some physical damage. Take it slowly at first, and work your way up.

- Set goals and deadlines. It's easy to say, "I want to get in shape," but that's not specific. What do you want to accomplish, and by when? It helps to set separate deadlines for different goals—some short-term and some longer-term—so that you can stay on track without overwhelming yourself. For example: "This week I will go for at least two walks" and "In six months I want to lose ten pounds and have more energy." This takes the big picture and divides it into doable pieces.

- Have fun. The best way to change exercise from a burden to a habit is to do something you enjoy. Try new things like cycling or hiking or walking with friends. Mix it up occasionally to keep things interesting and to find the activities that are most enjoyable for you.

- Stick with it. Take your intention seriously, but be kind to yourself.

- Buddy up. If possible, find a friend who is willing to share your routine. This will serve two purposes: motivate you and keep you company while you get fit together. Again, the more you enjoy your fitness routine, the more likely you are to stick with it.

My Fitness Game Plan

The iceberg beliefs I hold about fitness that I need to melt are:

I will melt them by doing this:

The iceberg beliefs I hold about fitness that I need to steer around are:

I will steer around them in these ways:

The iceberg beliefs I want to keep, but need to shave off the trouble spots for, are:

I will do that by using these mantras:

The negative thoughts that crop up for me when I am attempting to exercise are:

I will counteract those with the following thought zappers:

The fitness activities I will explore or begin are:

I will do that on these days, at these times:

The benefits I know I will get by developing and sticking to this plan are:

Day Ten

Strike a Work/Life Balance

Q *The Payoff: Smoother handling of the competing demands in your life*

"Balance? Ha! Forget it. The only thing in my life that's balanced is the amount of time I spend worrying about my work or my kids and the amount of time I spend worrying that I forgot to worry about something."   —Celeste, forty-nine

"The greatest source of stress for me is when I have to choose between the work I need to get done and spending time with my wife and kids. It invariably leads to frustration, which, ironically, I vent as anger at the kids. My goal is to have good-quality time with them, so I end up really beating myself up over ruining that."   —Brian, forty-one

"I have no life. Honestly, I feel like all I do is work. I'm in a really competitive industry, and I need to put in this kind of effort to get ahead, but sometimes I look around at my friends who have husbands and families and wonder when I'll find the time to get around to that."   —Anne, thirty-two

If any of these hit home for you, you're in good company.

Our studies show that work/life imbalance is, by far, the environmental element that causes the most amount of distress for the greatest number of people. Almost two-thirds of our database report that balancing the competing demands of their work and personal lives causes them significant stress.

The tension of striking a satisfying balance between work and life can get very emotional: we feel frustrated when we can't do what we want or need, angry when someone takes up our time with tasks we don't want to do, and guilty when we're taking time away from where we think we should be.

We understand. Even more, we know why this happens . . . and we can help.

The Crux of the Conflict

When we ask people to identify the source of their work/life conflicts, inevitably they will point to their enormous workload weighed against the demands of family and the yearning for personal time. Both of these things, of course, require our time and attention—unfortunately, often at the same time.

The pull between work and personal life brings up big emotions: *big* anxiety, *big* frustration, *big* guilt, *big* shame. Big emotions, as you know, signal that iceberg beliefs are on the loose. Icebergs represent our deepest beliefs and reflect our fundamental values, so it makes sense that they would show up around our home life and livelihood.

When it comes to work/life balance, many of us develop icebergs that lead us to expect more of ourselves than we can reasonably accomplish. Some beliefs, such as "I must excel at everything I do," drive us to be perfect (an impossible target) and to be all things to all people (another impossible target, unless you have magical powers to clone yourself at will). Others are just plain outdated or inaccurate, like "Only weak people take time off." When two or more of our icebergs clash with each other, the stress sparks start flying.

Imagine if you had an iceberg belief that "A good mother is always there for her kids," along with "I must appear professional at work at all times." Now imagine you have a big meeting scheduled at work and your kid wakes up with a fever of 102. Can you envision the explosion of snow and ice as these two icebergs crash into each other? If you're someone who has similar icebergs to these, you don't have to work too hard to envision it because you've experienced the frustration, anxiety, and stress firsthand.

The Gender Gap

We've seen a preponderance of literature and debate in recent years about the issues women face with work/life balance. Andrew's studies in the United States, Europe, and Asia all reveal the same finding: women are no less resilient than men, yet they are struggling significantly more than men to keep these work/home worlds apart and find balance between them.

So what's up?

The difference is in the icebergs.

Icebergs, as you know, are inherited from our parents. Acclaimed psychologist Carol Gilligan's work shows that we do raise boys and girls differently. Girls are primed to be relationship nurturers, and boys to be achievement oriented. Beginning in grade school, a math failure is signaled by teachers as a major event for boys and of less concern for girls. On the other hand, unresolved conflicts between peers are more frowned upon in girls than boys. We're telling boys that success and work is their arena, and girls that the home is theirs, implicitly (or not so implicitly) sending them messages about what matters.

Fast-forward to a world in which women are entering the corporate world in record numbers and are highly motivated to achieve. There will be demands on their time that take them away from home life. For men with families, leaving their spouse and children behind to go to work is understood, accepted, and completely aligned with their achievement icebergs. But put a woman in that situation and it bucks our societal mores. A man with a high-profile sales job who travels around the country will be met with nods of approval for providing for his family. A woman in that same role may be met with subtle or not-so-subtle disapproval (her own included, possibly, if she has internalized early messages that it's her job to be there for her family, which is at odds with her drive to achieve).

On the surface of modern life, we've come to think differently about what a woman's role is. On a conscious level, we embrace women's drive to achieve; the problem is that many women have inherited subconscious icebergs that say otherwise. It's as if our deepest beliefs haven't yet caught up with what we now know to be acceptable.

To be fair, the pull to be in two places shows up for men, too. At the same time that we're seeing women flock to the achievement world, we're seeing men allowing the nurturing side of themselves to emerge, so they, too, are feeling guilt about not being there for their kids. Male or female, the bottom line is that many of us *want* to be in both places, but the time/space continuum dictates that we cannot.

For some people, striking a life balance may not be about

"home" necessarily. Young Millennials and others (like Celeste, whom you read about at the opening of this chapter) are out there trying to make a name for themselves and working very long hours. They have lots of pride in their achievements at work, but outside of that, they feel they have no life. And they're right. Many have no time to go to the gym, no dinners out with friends, no time to just wander and explore. All they do is work.

> "These days, the standard answer to 'How are you?' isn't 'fine' or 'good.' The answer is 'busy.' Busy is the new normal."
>
> —Jan

There's no question that being overextended is the new norm. Our work/life stress is exacerbated by the fact that it takes more work than ever to stay afloat—and with fewer guarantees for the long term that the ship will keep sailing in calm waters. Whether we are being asked to work harder because resources are stretched thin or we are getting less money and security for the same output, it boils down to feeling ever more overextended. Not for one instant do we take anything away from that reality.

So what's the solution?

We're going to take you through a process today to help you isolate the icebergs that are preventing you from balancing the priorities in your life. You *can* have a life outside of work and balance in your priorities, without giving up everything you've worked for. We'll show you how to shift away from feeling overwhelmed and to a clearer head space to be able to prioritize with more peace and calm.

MODERN WORLD, MODERN STRESS: Balancing the competing demands of life is indeed a tough issue. But as we've said before, the stickier the problem, the greater relief you get from solving it. meQuilibrium members who initially scored below the norm in this area were able to boost their ability to cope with competing demands by more than 20 percent—and that has a far-reaching impact beyond just daily relief. The ability to prevent our work lives and personal lives from bleeding into one another is one of the greatest predictors of overall resilience. So, not only do we gain the ability to focus on work in spite of problems at home and be truly engaged with our families when we are there—we also get the added bonus of greater stress management capability across the board.

. . . .

All Work and No Play

The primary question we're going to ask you to ask yourself with regard to extreme working habits is this: How are you compromising your other life goals by only channeling down one avenue?

Time is a zero-sum game. Unlike other scenarios in which you can find a win-win strategy, the time we put into our jobs we cannot spend with our families or in other pursuits, because it is a finite resource. We cannot spend it in two ways. The tricky thing about icebergs is that they can drive us to funnel that precious resource into our work at the expense of everything else we want to experience or achieve.

If you dial down at work, you may not get ahead as fast as you want. That's possible. But the key question is: Is that your only goal? What else matters to you in your life that you are sacrificing for this one avenue of achievement? Remember, time is zero-sum. So, what you really need to do is analyze how your icebergs are getting in the way of your investing it in *all* the ways you want to. See the situation accurately and you'll make clearer decisions, from the broadest perspective possible, rather than being pushed down one road unconsciously. Let's get these icebergs in our scope so that we can recognize when they are steering our ship, and navigate a beneficial path around them.

Leading with Your Heart to Quiet the Chaos

Values-driven leadership is not only the best way to lead; it is the only way to stay authentic and centered in the midst of work chaos. And, it's a highly successful way to manage your work/life conflict and improve your performance. When you're authentic and values-driven, you choose to align your actions with what you believe in. Those who are unsure end up reacting to stress rather than choosing their responses. They find themselves in sticky situations because they don't know who they are or whom they're trying to please.

On Day 12, you'll learn more about the skill of aligning your actions with your life goals. In the meantime, as you are looking today at the belief-driven decisions you make about work, it's helpful to ask yourself what you stand for. Why do you do the work you do? What do you hope to inspire in your team and in others? What is the legacy you are looking to impart, and are the choices of how you are showing up at work each day aligned with that?

Take Action

It's important to know that this is a practice, and the shift won't happen all at once. But the more you employ this skill, the more balance you'll achieve. Over time, the icebergs that no longer serve you will melt away, and you'll become surprisingly adept at spotting and navigating around the rest.

Here are your steps for striking a work/life balance:

Step One: Identify the Icebergs

What beliefs keep you chained to your desk or your computer, drafting table, or wherever else you do your work? Read through this list of common work icebergs (page 170) until you hit upon one that gives you that "Yes, that's true!" zing of recognition.

Moments of big emotionality are another good way to identify your work/life balance icebergs. Remember, if the emotional response you're having is disproportionate to the actual event at hand, it's a clue that an iceberg is lurking. When that happens, use your drill-down technique to unearth it. Find the automatic thought behind the powerful emotion you're feeling, and then ask yourself the four key questions:

1. What is the most upsetting part of that for me?
2. And what does that (my answer to #1) mean to me?
3. What is the worst part of that (my answer to #2) for me?
4. Assuming my answer to #3 is true, why is that so upsetting to me?

Common Icebergs Around Work

"I must appear professional at all times."

"Successful people juggle it all. If I can't, then I'm not successful."

"I must always deliver."

"I should lead by example."

"I need to be at work."

"It's my job to provide, so I have to step up."

"My children need to have x, y, z, so I need to work to be able to afford that."

"If I don't run things/do it myself, nothing will get done right."

"Only weak people need to take time off."

"If I take time off, I'll be seen as dispensable."

"I need to excel at everything I do."

"Important people work long hours."

Step Two: Determine Which Icebergs Need to Be Embraced (While Shaving Off the Trouble Spots)

Which icebergs do you want to keep that are still perhaps causing conflict in certain situations? A good example of this would be "I must always deliver." That's a noble work ethic, and one you may deem worth keeping. But if you get handed a project at the eleventh hour, and you don't have the materials you need to get it done, you're likely to crash into some pretty big emotions. That's the trouble spot you need to shave off.

Here is where a mantra will come in handy—something you tell yourself when you bump up against that familiar iceberg.

Then you can calmly solve the problem and do the damage control that's needed. Next time, instead of going ballistic or dissolving in tears, you can refuse to let the situation hijack your emotions and take something like this approach:

> *"Okay, I know I must be bumping up against my familiar iceberg of always needing to deliver. That's something I prize about myself, but in this circumstance, it's not possible. That doesn't mean I'm compromising my integrity or values; it just means **that I'm human and can only do what is humanly possible.***
>
> *I need a plan. First, I will e-mail my boss and calmly explain to him why this project can't get done tonight. But I will also tell him specifically what is still needed for me to do, and how and when I will be able to do it, and then give him a reasonable timeline for delivery."*

Let's look at a second example from a real life meQuilibrium member. Jennifer is a forty-year-old single working mom of a seven-year-old. She's a website developer who is making a good name for herself, and she needs to get a proposal to a prospective big client by Monday. The problem is that it's Sunday, and her son is looking up at her with big, blue, disappointed eyes when she tells him she can't play with him because she has to work for most of the day. Jennifer feels the stress begin to rise as anxiety takes hold and her thoughts began to spiral: "This is a mess. I need to get this work done—it could be a huge client for me that will bring in a lot of money—but how can I have my kid just play by himself all day? What kind of mother does that? I should be with him . . ."

There it was: the *should* that was Jennifer's clue that her icebergs of "I must step up to get ahead" and "A good mother should always be there for her kids" were colliding. Here's how she navigated them:

> *"Yes, I believe I need to continue to work hard to get ahead in this business. That's a value I want to keep. I also believe that a good mother should be there for her kids. Another value I want to keep. I have to remember that these are not necessarily mutually exclusive.* **Sometimes caring for my son means that I need to work to be able to provide for him.** *By doing this today, I can land the project that will enable me to afford his camp tuition, and that will benefit him. I will make a plan with him to work until 4:00 and then take him to the park. That will also motivate me to work more efficiently so that I can get this done and we can get out to play."*

And that's how we talk ourselves off the ledge of a rocky iceberg!

Step Three: Determine Which Icebergs Need to Be Melted
Which, from your list, are not serving you? Which are outdated or no longer useful to you? For which ones do the cons far outweigh the pros? For each one that needs to be melted, challenge them with a thought zapper that you will apply whenever you bump up against it. Here are a few to give you some ideas:

Iceberg Belief: "I need to be at work."
Ice Breaker: "Do I really 'need' to be at work, or do I 'choose' to be at work? I need to keep a job, but I don't always have to be the first one to arrive and the last to leave."

Iceberg Belief: "Only weak people take time off."
Ice Breaker: "That's not true. It takes more strength to prior-

itize things outside of work than it does to conform to this outdated idea."

Iceberg Belief: "Important people work long hours."
Ice Breaker: "That's nonsense. Important people don't work long, they work smart. I do not have to conform to the social

Working Hard vs. Working Smart

We promised you that we weren't going to tell you to work less in order to alleviate your stress, and we're sticking to that. How much you choose to work is up to you. The key word there, however, is *choose*. Stress comes not from how much we work, necessarily, but from how we respond to the internal and external pressures to put work above everything else in our lives.

Having said that, it's helpful to remember we live exactly once. For those who use up their days, hours, and years constantly working—especially if it's doing work that isn't meaningful or engaging—it nearly always leads to regret. (Patients facing terminal illnesses often lament having prioritized work above spending time with their loved ones.) While it may not seem like it from where you sit right this instant, *you do have choices about how you spend your time.* There may be more breathing space in your days—and hence in your life—than you are currently seeing.

Where are you taking on responsibilities at work that you don't necessarily need to? Where are you losing time to unimportant tasks? Where can you work smarter? And, more important, what iceberg beliefs surface when you ask yourself these questions?

pressure to work long hours. What can I adjust in my daily routine so that I am making better use of my time?"

Iceberg Belief: "Anything less than Supermom or Superdad is neglectful."
Ice Breaker: "Nonsense. Part of being a good parent means not being burned out and cranky."

Step Four: Determine Which Icebergs You Need to Maneuver Around
These don't necessarily warrant the expenditure of your time or energy to melt. For instance, an iceberg of "People shouldn't mix business and pleasure" will only come up around the time of the holiday party or company picnic, or when you're invited to a dinner at your boss's home or when a personal friend approaches you about collaborating on a professional matter.

Remember, this is a practice. Your work and family/home are likely two of the most important factors in your life, and learning to balance these is a lifelong pursuit. But with this skill, you now have the tools to identify and manage the internal conflicts that are at the heart of the struggle and to begin to make clearer, more informed choices about where, how, and with whom you spend your time and energy.

My Plan for Striking Work/Life Balance

I choose to work on this skill because:

The activities and pursuits I want to have more of in my daily life are:

The icebergs around work that I need to melt are:

I will melt those with these ice breakers:

The icebergs around work that I want to embrace but shave off the trouble spots from are:

I will use this mantra to do that:

The icebergs around work that I need to steer around are:

I will steer around them by:

Day Eleven

Get Unstuck

Q *The Payoff: Release from the knots and problems that confound you*

Where are you stuck?

Almost everyone has at least one problem in his or her life that feels unsolvable. What's the one that comes to mind for you, that's recurring or chronic? Maybe it's friction with your coworker or a repeated standoff with your child or a financial issue. Whatever it is, it's likely causing you significant stress. So let's help you break free of it. Today you're going to learn a powerful skill to unravel most—if not all—of the seemingly fixed knots in your life.

An Explanation . . . or Two . . . or Three . . .

A slew of data shows that when human beings are struck by any kind of adversity, we are hardwired to spontaneously seek the cause. We immediately ask, "Why is this happening?" We also reflexively answer that question. The problem is that we don't answer it objectively. We respond through the lens of our *explanatory style.*

An explanatory style is our way of making sense of what

happens in the world. These styles were identified by a team of psychologists—Lyn Abramson, Lauren Alloy, and Martin Seligman—while studying depression risk at the University of Pennsylvania in 1978. One style was "Me, Always, Everything" (which loosely translates to "It's my fault, and this character flaw affects all elements of my life, all the time), which clearly, even to a nonexpert's eye, is a thinking style that would put people at risk for depression. Then there was "Not Me, Not Always, Not Everything" (which translates to "Not my fault, this is a one-time occurrence, and it doesn't affect anything but this one thing"), which buffered a person against depression.

Andrew discovered that two subsets of these styles have the greatest impact on our ability to manage stress, because they hamper us from effectively solving problems. People with an **Always/Everything** explanatory style can make a situation seem less solvable than it really is, so they give up prematurely. That creates a mountain of chronically unsolved problems, and likely heaping helpings of frustration and shame: three things that are sure to load up your metaphorical seesaw in the negative direction.

EXPLANATORY STYLE: The causes we habitually point to as explanations for what happens to and around us in the world.

Others may have a **Not Always/Not Everything** style, which is stressful in a different way. That leads them to believe a problem is more solvable than it really is, so they waste valuable time and resources wrestling with something that's outside their control. In either case, they're upping their level of stress.

There is a third explanatory style that impacts stress: **Me/ Not Me**, which focuses on who you *believe* is to blame. Is the problem something you believe you generated, or is it something that happened because of others or circumstances outside of yourself?

A Me explanatory style can be empowering, because it puts the locus of control within you. You can do damage control or fix what needs fixing. You are taking responsibility for your destiny. The flip side of this, however, is that you may automatically blame yourself for any problems that come up, even when you're not the cause, loading up on sadness, guilt, shame, and embarrassment.

While the Me/Not Me element is less potent in terms of our ability to solve problems than the Always/Everything and Not Always/Not Everything factors, it's still helpful to note as you look at all sides of a problem's causes to mine for the most options for viable solutions.

Solving the Unsolvable

Just as with our emotion radars and icebergs, we tend to pick up our parents' mental models of explaining how the world is. And just as with your other thinking habits, you develop habits around your explanatory style. Because those habits are learned so early and deeply ingrained, when a problem comes up, you automatically attribute the causes according to whatever you've learned. The problem is that you're applying the same old tired thinking to the same recurring issue—not really a formula for breakthrough success.

The secret to getting unstuck is in understanding where your explanatory style is limiting you. Your explanatory style only allows you to see a narrow subset of causes of the problem. When you can only see a subset of causes, you can only see a subset of solutions. You're stuck because your explanatory style is blinding you to a whole array of other possible solutions. Like any thinking style, the key is to get it out of the subconscious so that you can evaluate it properly. Learn what your style is—and how to be flexible around it—and you unstick the problem.

> **EXPLANATORY STYLE AND RESILIENCE**: What makes someone resilient? When Andrew asks that question of audiences, the typical response is "They persevere." And in a way, that's right. But if you drill down, there's much more to the story. What makes one person persevere and another person give up? Many would say hope. Hope is a wonderful thing to have, but what makes one person have it when another does not? A person has hope because they still have possible solutions available to them; yet what makes one person run out of solution possibilities sooner than someone else? When they are stuck in their explanatory style, and only have a subset of causes and solutions in their view, they can only see what they can see, and are thus missing out on a whole array of other possibilities.

Are you getting bogged down under unsolvable problems because you have an Always/Everything style, and you're blind to those aspects over which you have control? Or do you have a Not Always/Not Everything style that's causing you to spin your wheels on a problem that you're convinced you can handle but that actually has large chunks of its cause outside your control?

Let's find out.

What's Your Explanatory Style?

Your style may not necessarily be an absolute Always or Not Always, Everything or Not Everything; what we're looking to discover is which way you tend to lean most often. Read the following scenarios, and note the first thing that flashes into your mind when you ask yourself why it happened:

Scenario #1: *You've put a few calls in to one of your friends, and she hasn't called you back. Why?*

Scenario #2: *You and your teenage daughter are arguing more than usual. Why?*

Scenario #3: *Your marriage doesn't have the physical intimacy it used to. Why?*

You probably had little or no problem answering those questions. How you answered depends on your explanatory style, which, as we've hinted, has three dimensions.

The Three Dimensions of Explanatory Style

Me vs. Not Me (I'm to blame vs. Someone/something else is at fault)

Always vs. Not Always (The cause is permanent/fixed vs. The cause is temporary/it will pass)

Everything vs. Not Everything (This affects all aspects of my life vs. This affects just this)

ME VS. NOT ME

Do you tend to blame yourself (Me) or other people or circumstances (Not Me)? Here are some examples:

Scenario #1: *One of your friends hasn't called you back.*
Me: *"I've done something to offend her."*
Not Me: *"She's busy."*

Scenario #2: *You and your teenage daughter have been arguing more lately.*
Me: *"I've been less patient with her lately."*
Not Me: *"She's going through a phase."*

Scenario #3: *Your marriage has lost physical intimacy.*
Me: *"I don't make time for him."*
Not Me: *"He doesn't make time for me."*

Are you more of a Me or a Not Me? You're probably thinking that it depends on the situation, and it does. But each of us has a default setting or bias toward one or the other. So again, consider the kind of thinker you are: Me or Not Me? Knowing this will help you see if you are falling into a personalizing or externalizing trap, and enable you to use your new skills to see the other side of things.

ALWAYS VS. NOT ALWAYS

When you think about a problem, do you tend to settle on causes that will be around for a long time or ones that will pass? Take a look at these examples:

Scenario #1: *One of your friends hasn't called you back.*
Always: *"She's insensitive and uncaring."*
Not Always: *"She's really under the gun these days."*

Since people don't tend to suddenly shift from caring to uncaring, the former has a more permanent feel about it, while the words *these days* hint at a temporary cause.

Scenario #2: *You and your teenage daughter have been arguing more lately.*
Always: *"Teenagers like to argue."*
Not Always: *"She's in the middle of final exams and feeling stressed out."*

The first sounds like an unchangeable rule: you have to simply accept the nature of teenagers until they grow out of it. The second is temporary: once exams end, the arguments will abate.

Scenario #3: *Your marriage has lost physical intimacy.*
Always: *"Intimacy has a shelf life. After a certain number of years, it's over."*
Not Always: *"We've both been distracted and tired lately."*

Again, the first is permanent: intimacy just ends. In the second, the word *lately* suggests a temporary state.

You can see how an Always explanatory style can get in the way of your ability to problem-solve and cause you a great deal of stress in the process. If you settle on an Always cause, you're saying, in essence, that the problem doesn't have a solution. This can lead to some pretty damaging feelings of helplessness and hopelessness. Dimmed sparks in the bedroom can be reignited with a little effort and creativity; a full-on loss of love is a whole other story. A friendship that isn't going well you can work on, but a flawed ability to get along with *anyone and everyone* is pretty pervasive.

What's your default? Are you more of an Always or Not Always?

EVERYTHING VS. NOT EVERYTHING

When you get hit by adversity, do you tend to focus on that specific problem or look for causes that spill into other dimensions and domains of your life?

> Scenario #1: *One of your friends hasn't called you back.*
> Everything: *"I'm not good with people."*
> Not Everything: *"I don't handle this friendship well."*

> Scenario #2: *You and your teenage daughter have been arguing more lately.*
> Everything: *"She's impossible."*
> Not Everything: *"She can't handle criticism well."*

You'll notice that in the Everything scenarios, there's a character judgment involved—of yourself or of someone else. It speaks to who they *are*, rather than something they *did*. "She's impossible" would extend to all aspects of dealing with your daughter, since that's how you are characterizing her. "She just can't handle criticism" is specifically about the cause of her actions in this one scenario.

> Scenario #3: *Your marriage has lost physical intimacy.*
> Everything: *"We've fallen out of love."*
> Not Everything: *"Physical intimacy becomes less important over time."*

Here you'll see, again, that the Everything cause spills out into all aspects of your relationships (how you relate, feel about each other, and so on), whereas the Not Everything explanation pertains to just the physical aspects.

The sticking point of settling on an Everything cause is that you're saying the problem is one that exists in many areas of your life. This can lead you to think the problem is too big to manage. It's overwhelming to try to deal with a teenager you deem "impossible" on all fronts, but likely manageable to work with her on learning to take criticism better or to temper how and when you deliver it.

When Andrew works with children with the Always/Everything style, they often put their academic struggles down to "I'm stupid." He is greatly relieved when he hears this, because the broader the explanation (I'm stupid vs. I'm bad at math), the easier it is to disprove and dispel. For instance: Does the child play computer games? Yes? Great. What's his favorite game? What level has he made it to on that game? Ah, super pro expert. Hmm, then, he can't be stupid if he can master something that complex, can he? Neither Andrew nor the child can solve "stupid." But they certainly can make some headway

How to Spot "Always" and "Everything" Thoughts

- Always thoughts typically contain the words *never* or *always*, or they are about long-term personality and character flaws or fundamental talents and abilities. For instance, "I always order the wrong thing on the menu" or "I'm hopeless at math."

- Everything thoughts cut across many avenues in your life, not just the one situation with which you're dealing. For instance, "I can't fix this leaking tap because I'm an idiot."

on study habits or powers of concentration or even mental blocks to math.

The fact is, most problems have a myriad of causes. But in the midst of trying to solve a sticky problem, particularly when we're feeling down or stressed, we tend to see only the Always and Everything, which are the things we can't solve. The trick is to train yourself to recognize the Always and Everything explanations in your head, set them aside, and focus instead on the Not Always and Not Everything causes to unearth more and better solutions. Remember, the more causes you can see, the more resolutions you have available to you.

Take Action

Okay, let's put this skill to work for you. Follow these steps to get unstuck.

1. Choose one problem in your life that feels unsolvable. That's the one we're going to tackle. Let's say, for instance, that you have an employee who is particularly difficult to deal with. He's making mistakes and generally causing headaches for you. Write down the problem.

2. Identify why you think this is happening. Why is this difficult dynamic happening? What or who is the cause? Go with whatever the immediate thought is that comes into your head. It doesn't have to just be one cause; list up to three of what you believe are the major causes of this problem. Write them down. Let's say your answers are: *He never listens to what I'm telling him* and *He's incompetent.*

3. Notice any Always or Everything causes in your answers, and circle them. While these could be real causes of your problem, they will lead you to a problem-solving dead end. Clearly, "He never listens to what I'm telling him" is an Always cause, and "He's incompetent" is an Everything cause, because it's a character indictment that extends way beyond this particular situation.

4. Now come up with as many Not Always and Not Everything causes as you can for the problem. The goal here is to generate as many possible *changeable* causes as possible. The table below lists some common Always and Everything explanations and their counterparts to give you some ideas. For the situation with your employee, you might change your "He never listens" to "He isn't listening to what I'm telling him about this project." "He's incompetent" could, instead, be seen as "He's not strong in these particular areas." Can you see how you've now reframed them as solvable problems, rather than morasses of stuck-ness?

ALWAYS/EVERYTHING	NOT ALWAYS/NOT EVERYTHING
"She is irresponsible."	"She was careless in this situation."
"He doesn't care about me."	"He didn't ask me how my big presentation went today."
"She's not good with deadlines."	"She didn't meet this particular deadline."
"Everything is going wrong."	"I'm having difficulty with these specific things right now."

5. Come up with new solution strategies aligned with your Not Always and Not Everything causes. For instance, with your employee a new strategy might be "I will partner him with someone who is strong in this particular area, so they can work together to get the project done, and hopefully he can learn from this person for future projects."

> **FOR THE "NOT ALWAYS/NOT EVERYTHING" TYPES:** If you tend to have a Not Always/Not Everything style, you'll likely have far fewer instances where you get stopped by Always/Everything thoughts. At the same time, if you're stuck on a problem, it means you're also likely not seeing all causes and hence solutions to it. It can be helpful for you to generate some Always and Everything causes to identify if there are factors over which you truly have no control and that you need to accept with grace or to work around.

Learning to discriminate between solvable and unsolvable problems takes practice. But over time, you'll naturally start to see bright new solution possibilities for tired old problems. With this skill, you can untangle the knots in life that before seemed impossible. Now *that's* a breakthrough!

My Plan for Getting Unstuck

I choose to work on this skill because:

My default explanatory style is:

The unsolvable problem I want to break through is:

The immediate causes of this problem I see are:

The Always and Everything elements of those explanations are:

Conversely, I can come up with these Not Always and Not Everything explanations:

Based on the Not Always and Not Everything causes, I can apply these new solutions:

Day Twelve

Live Your Life Goals

The Payoff: A sense of purpose and passion in your everyday life

John Lennon once famously said, "Life is what happens to you while you're busy making other plans." That's true . . . but it needn't be. You can bring your life goals and your daily actions into alignment. That's what today's skill is about.

Much of our stress stems from the gap between our plans for the future and our behaviors today. For instance, "I want to get in shape, but I'm eating too much and not exercising and not doing anything to change that" or "I want to have a great career but I'm stuck in this dead-end job." We're busy checking off things on our daily to-do list, but we're rarely stopping to think about our bigger life goals. Overlooking this big picture takes a huge toll on our sense of fulfillment.

> "One of the biggest drags on us is being missionless. 'Blah' is our worst enemy."
>
> —Andrew

The three of us see this dynamic show up often: Adam sees it in his patients, for whom having a life purpose can make the difference between healing or suffering. Andrew sees it in his clients who feel adrift and "blah" because they are acting in ways that are either not advancing their life mission or are actively contradicting it. And in both her personal and work domains, Jan sees countless men and women who are so determined to get ahead for either financial gain or status that they lose sight of why it matters and, more important, how their work contributes to the bigger picture.

Our everyday lives are so hectic, and in truth, we kind of allow them to be. It's not easy to stop and take a breather and think about our bigger life plan, let alone act in ways that further it. But, spiritual beliefs aside, we only live once. If we don't make the most of it, we don't get another chance. When it comes to our overall experience of life, one of the best things we can do for the sake of our well-being and our contentment is to infuse our life—and our actions—with a sense of purpose and meaning.

> **THE POWER OF PURPOSE:** In our online program, we ask beginning participants to rate how much they believe that each of us has a meaning and purpose or can find that meaning and purpose. Those who rate lowest on this are half as able to deal with stress as those who rate highest. The good news: Looking at those who rated lowest, the program more than doubled their sense of meaning and purpose and increased their ability to manage their stress by a whopping 40 percent.

Adam tells the story of a patient in her early fifties who was experiencing back and neck pain. In his consultation with her, it came out that her mother had recently passed away. She was dealing with real grief, and that was exacerbating her physical complaints (emotional pain can trigger inflammation in the body). She had cared for her mother for a long time, and for the better part of a decade, that was what had made her life meaningful. Now that her mother had passed, she felt adrift and without purpose. She was grieving not just for the loss of her mother but for her loss of identity as a caretaker.

This patient was missing a key component of healing. If she wanted to feel better, she had to address her wellness on all levels, not just the physical. She needed to become whole again. She could—and did—try acupuncture for the pain, and some gentle exercises, but the bigger goal was for her to figure out what would make her life feel purposeful again. She needed to make some plans to find a sense of meaning and take steps to make it happen. Adam suggested she look into volunteer work in which she could use her compassion and skills to care for others.

Where do you want to be in twenty years? What kind of work do you want to be doing? If you'll no longer be working then, what do you want to spend your days doing? What kind of relationship do you want to have with your kids, your friends, your significant other? Where do you want to be living? And, even more important, are you acting in accordance with those life goals?

If you are, that's fantastic news. Keep going. If you sense a gap between what you want your life to be and what you're currently doing, then keep reading. We have some tools that can help.

Take Action

1. Define your goals. The first step in aligning your actions with your life mission is to identify what that mission is. Take some time today to look over the questions in the

box that follows and write out your answers to the ones that matter to you. Any that don't apply to your life, skip over. For ones that do matter to you, be as detailed as you can in your envisioning.

2. Choose one thing you want most. Look over your list. What feels the most urgent and desirable to you? What do you really want in your life, starting now? Do you want more meaningful work? Better connection to your spouse? To find the love of your life? A home? For now, ignore any automatic thoughts from your feed that pop up to derail you and convince you that you can't achieve or have these things (remember, you now have the tools to zap those).

3. Take one small step. Come up with just one five-minute activity you can do to move that forward. If it's a home you're dreaming of, perhaps you can call a real estate agent to schedule an appointment to see what's out there. If you want to feel more connected to your extended family, choose one family member to reach out to today. Commit to doing this one activity today and see what happens.

4. Use the positive momentum to keep going. Take note of how you feel after you take this step. Proud? Accomplished? Motivated? If so, commit to a day and time that you will do another five-minute step, either toward this goal or another one on your list. The more of these small steps you take, the more momentum you'll gain—and the more you will align what you do with what you want in life.

Here's how meQuilibrium member Lauren, forty-eight, put this into action:

"In twenty years, I want to have established enough success in my job to be able to leave the corporate world and work on my own as a consultant. I want to be able to set my own hours and travel often with my husband, who, by that time, will be retired. The one thing I will do, starting today, is to begin to strengthen my connections in my industry so that I have independent relationships with clients. I will also reach out to a

My Life in 20 Years

- What do I want my work life to look like? What do I want to have accomplished, and what do I want to be doing?

- What do I want to have in my romantic life? Who am I with, and what is our relationship like?

- What do I want my relationship with my children to be like?

- How do I want my children to be in the world? What qualities do I hope to have instilled in them?

- What do I want for my health?

- Where do I want to be living?

- Who do I want to be surrounded by?

- What creative, physical, or other endeavors do I want to have become accomplished in?

- What do I want to be known for in my community?

- What contribution do I want to have made to the world at large?

consultant I know to ask if I can take her to lunch and inter-view her about how she built her client base."

And here's the game plan that Todd, thirty-four, laid out:

"In twenty years, I want to be married with a few kids, living in a house that's close to my brother and his family. I want to be in good health and in good shape so that I can enjoy a weekly squash game with my buddies and be an active, engaged dad. But right now, I'm spending all my time at work and not social-izing, which will make it hard to meet the life partner that will make this plan work. So, the first step I will take is to tell my friend's girlfriend to go ahead and set me up with some of her friends like she's been asking me to let her do!"

Now it's your turn. What's your plan?

My Plan to Live My Goals

Here is what I want my life to look like in twenty years:

Here is one thing I want to bring into my life that is aligned with one of those goals, starting today:

Here is one thing I will do to move that forward:

I will do that on this day, at this time:

After I completed that step, I felt:

I will follow up that step with this next one:

Day Thirteen

Energize Your Work

The Payoff: Deeper satisfaction with your job

When most people think about stress at work, they think of a schedule crammed with tight deadlines, demanding projects, or a highly political environment. But those aren't the only sources of work stress.

Your work can also be stressful if, well, you don't like it. If you're not connected to your work, it's not a source of fulfillment and meaning, and that can make going to work every day a real drag. If, like many people, you spend eight hours or more a day working, this stress can also build up and spill into the rest of your life. If you aren't happy in your work life, it casts a real pall over everything else.

The good news is that you can turn this around—without having to quit your day job. We can show you the secret to finding contentment and fulfillment, no matter what kind of work you do.

Work and Connection

In 2006, Andrew was tasked by the Brookings Institution (a Washington, DC, think tank) to unravel one of their most perplexing psychology puzzles. They were researching job satisfaction and happiness in government employees, and a strange inconsistency kept popping up. Thirty years of research clearly showed that when it comes to job satisfaction, the same ten factors crop up again and again—things like good pay, good benefits, having autonomy, being able to rely on a stable budget, and so on. Any way they reviewed the data, though, they found that federal government employees were light on those common factors. Yet time and again, they also saw that these employees were significantly more satisfied with their jobs than their peers. How could this be?

Andrew set out to crack this nut and quickly discovered that not only were these people more satisfied in their jobs but overall they scored quite high on resilience. Did their satisfaction boost their resilience, or did their resilience make them more satisfied with their work? Or was there a third variable that was rising both tides, as Andrew suspected? It was a conundrum he could not untangle until he met a man named Steve Craft.

Steve was born in a very frosty part of northern Illinois. He graduated high school with great grades and some college offers. But Steve just wasn't ready for more school, so instead of college he got a job driving a tractor. The plan was to spend a year doing this, make some money, and then go to school. Somehow, ten years slipped by, until one day, sitting on that tractor in the dead of winter, Steve had an epiphany.

"I realized: I don't need to do this anymore," Steve recalls. He decided in that moment that he was going to become a rocket scientist. Steve is now a deputy director at NASA.

"So why NASA?" Andrew asked. "Why not go to the private sector where you'd make more money?"

"I interviewed in all those places," Steve said. "But NASA was the only place that said I wouldn't have to wear a tie to work."

Andrew laughed, but he knew there had to be more, so he pressed. Why stay with NASA even now, when he could go anywhere he wanted and cash out, live a cushy life?

"I thought about it," Steve replied. "But I'll never leave NASA, because I wake up every morning knowing that I am contributing to the welfare of my nation."

There it was: having a deep sense of meaning and purpose was what fueled Steve's job satisfaction—and the job satisfaction of thousands of other government employees.

After that, Andrew went on to ask thousands of people why they stay in their jobs. The answers fell into three buckets, or three levels.

The higher you go on the level of job connection, the greater your job satisfaction. Even better, this connection is a stress fighter: the greater your connection to your work, the better you cope with stressful situations and the day-to-day pressures of the job. It creates a resilience that changes how you see "stressful" work situations, transforming them into just "intense" work situations. Nothing more, nothing less. In other words, they demand your talents, energies, and focus—but they no longer force you to sacrifice your equilibrium in the process. As you see, it's in your best interest to be as connected to your job as you can.

So what's the secret? How do we move up in level? That's easy. The key to connection is to find your contribution.

The Three Levels of Work Connection

Level One: I'm here for the pay and benefits.

Level Two: I need the pay and benefits, but I also like the work, the challenge it presents, and my colleagues.

Level Three: I need the paycheck, I like the work and my colleagues, but there's something else. I feel that what I do contributes to something larger than myself: my organization, my industry, my community, my nation, or humanity.

What's Your Contribution?

Only about 30 percent of people naturally make it to a Level Three connection. Why do you think so few engage with their jobs in that way?

The truth is that you can't feel connected to your job if you can't see your contribution. Your contribution is exactly what it sounds like: what your work brings to the good of your organization, your colleagues, your nation, or the world at large. Your work might include such mundane tasks as posting sales data, answering customers' questions, explaining how your technology works, cataloging paperwork, or even just answering the telephone. But within all these tasks is a larger purpose—a Level Three reason for being at your job. It's just a matter of finding it, focusing on that contribution as you do your work, and celebrating it.

Take Olivia, for instance. Olivia is twenty-three and just starting out in the fashion industry. Her job as an entry-level intern involves sorting piles of fabric and supplies, and collating tear sheets. It's not the most exciting work, to say the least. But Olivia has a great attitude about it. Even at her young age, she tapped into the importance of knowing her contribution. She says:

> "Look, I know that ordering safety pins and sorting the blue silk from the periwinkle isn't glamorous, but what I do enables the designers to have easy access to the materials they need to create beautiful garments. When I watch the fashion shows or see our stuff in magazines, I get a little boost of pride because I know that I played even a tiny role in making that happen."

Take Action

To boost your connection level at work, today we're going to help you find all the Level Three reasons you do your job. Spend some time today asking yourself why you do the work you do. What is your unique contribution? What greater good do you serve by doing your work? In the box below are what some past meQuilibrium members have come up with.

Now it's your turn. Write down as many Level Three reasons as you can for your job. Make sure they are concrete and specific, and that you really believe them. Consider how your job contributes to the greater good, the next generation of your organization, or your company's mission. You might need to look beyond the obvious. One woman who worked as a cashier at a fast-food company whose products she didn't feel particularly good about did, however, embrace the company's well-known philanthropy efforts. So for her, every meal she sold meant more resources for sick children and other worthy charities.

When you have your complete list, put it in your phone, in your written notes, on your computer—anywhere handy and

Level Three Connections

- "I believe in what my company stands for, and I enjoy trying to make a difference within the company."

- "I am a voice of reason for people in my organization. I contribute a valued perspective."

- "I motivate people in my department to do their best work."

- "My work is meaningful because it makes a difference in the well-being of many people who use our products."

- "I help bring beauty to people and make them feel good about themselves."

- "I am the person customers see when they come through our doors. I represent the face of our company."

- "Through my work, I give people financial peace of mind."

- "I am making a difference for children by engaging their minds and imaginations."

- "I help spread joy."

- "I make it possible for many of our employees to earn good salaries and support their families."

- "I am mentoring the younger generation of our company."

visible. Every Monday morning and every Friday before you leave work, read through this list—and do so any other time that work starts feeling like a grind rather than a gift you are offering to the world. Over time, your list may change and grow, and you'll start to feel more deeply connected to your work. Don't just scan the list. Linger on every point. Think about the good you do, and take it to heart.

What you do really does matter. When you look at your work that way, it can go from being the ultimate drag to one of the most fulfilling, energizing lifts in your life.

My Plan for Energizing My Work

I choose to work on this skill because:

My unique contributions to my organization, industry, or the greater good are:

I will put this list in the following place so that I remember to read it often:

Day Fourteen

Connect to Something More

Q   *The Payoff: Reinfuse your life with meaning and joy*

What sustains you?

What gives your life meaning?

Those are the questions we're looking at today. When it comes to cultivating a deep reserve of resilience and calm to sustain us through life's choppy waters, we need to be moored to something greater than ourselves.

Connecting to something greater than ourselves gives us direction. It makes our lives so broad that it renders the daily trials and tribulations nearly insignificant. This deep-rooted connection provides motivation, turning dreaded tasks into effortless or even joyful execution of plans. If you're lit up with passion and purpose, life just feels easier. You feel fulfilled, happier, and more alive. Connection heals us.

Valerie, age fifty, is an artist

> "Just as in integrative medicine, we don't just want to get you to 'not sick.' The goal is to get you to the place of overall well-being that you want for yourself."
>
> —Adam

who suffered from back pain. The pain was preventing her from painting, so Valerie decided to have surgery to correct a herniated disk. The surgery was a success. About eight months later, Valerie came in to see Adam for an office visit. She reported that she had been doing relatively well, but not as well as she had hoped. The pain was gone, but she was a little lethargic and depressed. Adam asked her if she had started painting again, and she admitted that she hadn't. She and her husband had moved a few months back, and she hadn't bothered to set up her supplies in the new house.

Adam's prescription for Valerie was clear: go home and set up that studio. Valerie's artwork was how she expressed herself and how she felt complete. She wasn't going to feel healed until she put that sense of meaning and purpose back in her life.

The Levels of Life Fulfillment

Yesterday you learned about how to connect to your work for greater fulfillment. But is work all there is? No, of course not. After his discovery about the three levels of work connection, Andrew continued his research, knowing that only one in ten thousand people would say that their job is what gives them the deepest sense of meaning. He discovered there are four levels of life connection that sustain us. The higher people went, the greater their resilience and life satisfaction.

The Four Levels of Life Connection

It's easy to see why moving from Level One to Level Two would bring you great benefit. You're going beyond the surface stuff of life (the work presentation that went well, this quarter's earnings, and so on) and reaching outside yourself to engage with people close to you, for whom you care deeply. The love, safety, and sense of belonging we can get from our families can be profoundly nourishing. Having strong, fulfilling relationships with people we love is invaluable for our emotional well-being. In addition to being a lift that helps us achieve balance, having close personal relationships also has physiological benefits. Human touch stimulates oxytocin, the "cuddle hormone" that diminishes our experience of fear and floods our systems with a sense of calm. Not to mention that close relationships are a two-way street: we are supported, and we support those we love. They feed our sense of self-esteem.

We're not taking away one iota of the value of family life for your happiness and well-being. At the same time, the incontrovertible data show that we need to move higher to cultivate the rock-solid resilience that supports us through whatever happens in life.

Level Three is the next step. This includes the world around you, outside of your home. It involves an engagement with your community, social life, clubs, activities—whatever you do that is rewarding and that connects you with people you enjoy being with. On Level Three, we get all kinds of the positives we're looking to load up on: the pride of altruism we get from volunteering, the fun of being with friends whose company we enjoy, the zing of interest and engagement we get from joining in group activities we love. All good stuff. And yet, there's a deeper place we can go.

Level Four brings with it a bounty of resilience. The hallmark of Level Four is having a connection to something eternal, something that was here before you were born and will be here long after you leave. That litmus test is easiest filled by spirituality, faith, and religion, but that's not the case for everyone. There are many other avenues of Level Four connec-

> ## The Four Levels of Life Connection
>
> - Level One: Personal Goals. This is the arena of personal advancement. Goals are motivating and in many ways healthy, but some people focus almost exclusively on their own individual advancement.
>
> - Level Two: Family. Most of us extend our circle of connection around our family, especially our spouse and children. For the people on this level, family gives their lives the most meaning.
>
> - Level Three: Community. In addition to individual goals and family connections, this circle also includes community: volunteering, doing charity work, or otherwise contributing to society.
>
> - Level Four: Spirituality. Those who reach the widest circle of connection are tapped into something much bigger than themselves, their families, and even their immediate communities. These connections reflect a person's own brand of spirituality, such as religious faith, a communion with the natural environment, or a set of enduring values.

tion, as well. It could be a meaningful bond with nature or an enduring set of values like fighting for equality, aiding the less fortunate, or protecting the environment. Really, it's anything that taps us into the greater realm of humanity.

For Ed, sixty-two, his Level Four connection came through his military experience. A proud member of the Marine Corps, Ed embodies the motto Semper Fidelis (always loyal). He lives and breathes the Marine Corps values of courage, honor, and commitment, and this is how he approaches his relationships with colleagues, neighbors, and strangers. He embodies the proud tradition of the Corps, and is guided and sustained by these values that were upheld by marines long before he was born and will be held high by subsequent generations long after he's gone.

When Life Gets Tough, the Tough Get Connected

It may seem counterintuitive to add things to your life when you're feeling stressed. But when times are toughest, resilient people instinctively know they need to broaden their connections. It makes them feel better, it makes them stronger people, it shields them against stress . . . and it does others good, too.

The irony is that just when we need these connections the most, like when we are very stressed, is often when we pull inward. Right when we should reach out to boost our resilience, we shrink back. We contract. We quit sitting on boards, stop volunteering, and instead stay home and watch videos and eat popcorn.

During the Great Recession, Andrew located a group of people across the world who had been hit the hardest by economic strife but who were, surprisingly, testing through the roof on resilience. He dubbed them "The Marathon Club" because of their hardiness. These people had lost their homes and their jobs, and many were living hand to mouth, but somehow, they never lost their faith that they would pull through. What united these people was that they all instinctively knew to reach out to others when things were at their worst.

There was Brandon, a young man from Albany, New York, who had just graduated with his master's when the recent recession hit. He sent off four hundred job applications, with no success. His wife, Amanda, had been guaranteed a teaching job but was told that the person who was vacating that position decided not to leave with the economy being what it was. The odds felt stacked against them. But Brandon and Amanda decided to do the one thing that was calling out to them, rather than worry about their prospects. Breast cancer was prevalent in his family, and he had become aware that women of his generation were at special risk because they weren't getting screened. So the couple went out on the road, from state to state, using social media to gather crowds together and educating people on the importance of early detection. They called it their "Kick Breast Cancer's Butt Tour." Brandon's life might have not been exactly as he wanted it to be at that point in life, and yet he scored off the charts on life satisfaction because he was connected to a greater purpose.

There were Roxanne and Peter, a couple who had lost their home and their jobs during this time. They were living on disability, down to their last pennies. With just enough money left for one tank of gas, they decided to spend that tank of gas driving to a memorial service for the family of Don Yoon, whom they had never met. Don Yoon's wife and young children were killed when a fighter jet crashed into their house in the San Diego suburbs, and Roxanne and Peter had seen his despair when he was interviewed on television. Something prompted them to reach out to this man in need, even though they themselves were scraping rock bottom. Like Brandon and Amanda, though their circumstances appeared bleak, their outlook was bright, and their life satisfaction and resilience sky-high.

Things don't need to be at their worst to make this skill worthwhile. Just like you don't want to learn to use a nail gun the day you're building your house, you want to master the tools of connection long before you need them.

Let's get you more connected.

Take Action

Statistically, you're probably at a Level Two, and that's a wonderful place to start. To expand your connection circle, you need to add community (Level Three) and spiritual (Level Four) connections to your life. Here's how.

EXPAND TO LEVEL THREE

Begin by thinking about your specific interests. Is there a particular population you'd like to help (e.g., kids, the elderly, single moms)? Is there a cause or goal you'd like to support (better schools, the environment, affordable housing, a political issue)?

Next, think about your talents. Are you good at organizing and managing people? Do you have teaching experience? Carpentry skills? Are you good with computers? Working with kids?

Now it's time to find a place to combine your interests and your talents. Ask people you know or do a web search for organizations in your area that cover your interest and require your skills. Maybe your local Habitat for Humanity needs help building affordable housing for struggling families. Perhaps disadvantaged kids at a nearby school need a math tutor, or your local animal shelter needs volunteers. Maybe you can gather a few friends to make sandwiches for a local homeless shelter, or join together to organize a Neighborhood Watch program. Maybe you can collect signatures to get your political cause on the ballot. Chances are you won't have to look very far to find a way to engage.

The last step: Do it. That's all there is to it. Reach out and become part of a bigger circle and watch what happens.

EXPAND TO LEVEL FOUR

For Level Four connections, the answer lies within you. Only you know what calls to you. Are you looking for artistic expression through music, art, or literature? Perhaps an easy first step would be to visit an art gallery or join a book club where you can discuss with others the eternal human themes that make great literature. Or, if you haven't visited your faith or religion since your childhood, why not take it off the shelf, dust it off, and see what elements of that faith still fit with the person you are now? If you feel at home in nature, perhaps now is the time to plan a day hike or even just a walk in the woods. There are so many options with Level Four. The key is to attach to something truly eternal that resonates for *you*.

As you've traveled through these 14 days, you've learned a lot. You've mastered so many skills, from emotion regulation to problem-solving, taking back your time to making the healthy lifestyle changes that buffer you against stress. You've loaded up on the good stuff to dial your life into the positive, and here, today, you're sealing the deal. You're ensuring that your days to come will be held steady by the skills you've mastered and anchored by a greater sense of meaning and purpose.

While we can't promise that life won't throw you a curveball or two, we can promise that you'll be very ready and able to field it when that curveball comes.

My Plan to Connect to Something More

I choose to work on this skill because:

The Level Three connection I will cultivate is:

I will do that in these specific ways:

The Level Four connection I will cultivate is:

I will do that in these specific ways:

THREE
Keep It Going

4

Life, in Balance

You now have the basic training for getting your life under control. You've learned how to calm your emotions, unlock your problem-solving power, and root out faulty thinking and hidden beliefs that trip you up. You're armed with the essential tools to keep your work, home, and personal life in balance, to take care of yourself physically, and to boost your stress-busting resilience by loading up on the positive.

But it doesn't end there.

The best part of this program is that these skills can be applied to any and every area of your life going forward. From clearing your clutter to repairing a relationship rut, you can apply what you know to make fast and lasting changes.

For instance:

If You Are Stuck on a Problem...

Stop. Think. You now have two potent skills at your disposal to get unstuck from even the knottiest problem.

First, ask yourself: Who is to blame for the problem? To what are you attributing the cause? Feeling stuck is a sign that your explanatory style may be limiting your view. You may only be seeing a subset of causes and, hence, a subset of possible solutions. Use the skills you learned on Day 11 to identify your explanatory style and get flexible with it to smoothly untangle the problem.

If the problem that's confounding you is one that feels familiar to you—if you've been here before—it's a clue that you may have fallen into a thinking trap. Remember, we can make our problems seem more insurmountable than they really are through habitual faulty thinking. Use the skills you learned on Day 3 to identify and escape the trap that's got you in its grip.

If You Have Difficulty Focusing . . .

Are you sleeping well? The physical is the first place to look if you're having focus issues; exhaustion can cloud our thinking in a big way. Be honest with yourself. Are you getting your optimal amount of sleep every night? Are your evening habits helping or hindering your efforts? Remember, without good sleep, it's almost impossible to employ any of the other basic skills you've learned here. Apply your Sleep Smart skills to get the rest you need to feel refreshed and sharp.

If lack of sleep isn't the culprit, check your emotion radar. Remember, negative emotions make it difficult to concentrate on anything but how bad you feel. Check in with your physical signals to determine what you're feeling. Are you getting bogged down by anger, anxiety, frustration, guilt, embarrassment, or shame? Use your TMZ skill to root out the thoughts generating the negative emotion and zap it if it isn't warranted.

Lastly, for a quick fix, try one of your skills from Day 4 to access instant calm: deep breathing, progressive muscle relaxation, or positive imagery. All three are equally useful when you need to regain your focus, as they automatically shut down the sympathetic nervous system that, when chronically activated, obscures our thinking, scatters our focus, and blunts our powers of concentration.

If You Feel Overwhelmed . . .

You're out of balance, which means it's time to recalibrate the ratio of good and bad in your life. Go through the steps you learned on Day 7 to banish the burnout: ditch the drudge, reframe the required, add in the good stuff, and do active accounting to restore the balance in your favor.

If You Feel Run-Down . . .

Again, start with the most obvious place: the physical. If you aren't nourishing your body with good sleep, healthy food, and exercise, you're bound to feel run-down. Use your Sleep Smart, Refuel the Right Way, and Find Your Fitness Fault Lines skills to get yourself back on track.

Beyond the physical, feeling run-down signals that you may also be depleted emotionally. The good news is that you have the cure for that: tune in to your positive radars. Use the skills you learned on Day 8 to tap into the Big 6 positive emotions: happiness, pride, interest/engagement, esteem/respect, love, and contentment. Give yourself the lift that will invigorate you and boost your resilience.

If You're Stuck in a Relationship Rut . . .

Yes, you can even use these skills to get your partnership out of a chronically bad spot. For some, it's the little stuff that causes big friction, like arguments over household chores. For others, the hot spots are bigger, like disagreements over money or life plans. We dig ourselves in deep by repeating these patterns of conflict.

If you feel frustrated in your relationship, take a look and see if you've fallen into a mind-reading trap. Have you assumed you know what your partner is thinking, without asking? Are you expecting your partner to know what you're thinking or hoping for, without having clearly communicated that?

If this trap has appeared for you, use your TMZ skill. Here's how:

1. Trap the emotion. The first step is to know when you're mind reading. The telltale sign is frequently feeling frustrated or angry with someone for not meeting our wants and needs.

2. Map the emotion to the thoughts behind it. Ask yourself, "Why am I frustrated? What did I expect? What did I need?" Then ask yourself the tough question: "Did I actually ask for it?" If the answer is no, then you're in a mind-reading trap.

3. Zap it. How? By saying something—out loud! If you're not sure that you've expressed something, speak up. Repetition can't hurt.

If You Are Having Difficulty Changing a Habit...

Those are icebergs in your way—whether it's clearing out your clutter, getting to the gym regularly, or choosing herbal tea over extralarge whipped mocha drinks. Remember, lifestyle changes can't be made on the behavioral level if you don't first root out the hidden beliefs that are tripping you up. Use your skills from Day 6 to discover the icebergs that are derailing your efforts and to determine whether you need to melt them, shave off trouble spots, or steer around them.

If You Feel "Blah"...

It's time to get connected! "Blah" is the polar opposite of feeling inspired, and we feel inspired when we're infused with a sense of meaning and purpose.

If your professional life is feeling like a drag rather than a lift, review your skills from Day 13 to find the deeper *why* behind what you do and to reenergize your work.

To infuse our lives beyond work, we need to widen our circle. Most people have a Level Two connection to family, and that's an excellent place to start. But for greater resilience, we need to go bigger. Remember, the bigger your boat, the less likely you are to capsize. Level Three reaches out to your community, connecting you to the world around you. This level includes volunteering, doing charity work, or otherwise contributing to society.

Level Four is the deepest wellspring of resilience: a connection to something universal and lasting. The key is to connect to something that was here long before you were born and will remain long after you leave this planet: nature, spirituality, religion, a code of ethics, and so on. What sustains you? What serves as your guiding star? Review Day 14's skills for connection to something more to banish the blah fast, and for good.

This is just the beginning. We invite you to go to www .mequilibrium.com and become part of our community to learn ways to continue to put your basic training to excellent use in everyday life.

Yes, life can be stressful. There's no denying that. But now you know exactly what to do in the face of it. You have what it takes to go from overwhelmed to in control, from burned out to in balance. Most important, you can use what you know to ensure that your days are filled with meaning, peace, and joy.

Isn't that what life is all about, after all?

Index